COMBATTING MENTAL HANDICAP

A Multidisciplinary Approach

Social and Environmental Factors in the Prevention and Amelioration of Mental Handicap

Edited by
Peter L. C. Evans
Institute of Education, London
and
Alan D. B. Clarke
University of Hull, UK

A B ACADEMIC PUBLISHERS

Published in the UK by
A B Academic Publishers
P O Box 42
Bicester
Oxon OX6 7NW

British Library Cataloguing in Publication Data

Combatting mental handicap: a multidisciplinary approach:
Social and environmental factors in the prevention and
amelioration of mental handicap.
1. Man. Mental retardation. Prevention
I. Evans, Peter   II. Clarke, Alan
616.858805

ISBN 0-907360-15-7

Printed in Great Britain

COMBATTING MENTAL HANDICAP

Contents

This is the first of a series of books on various Multidisciplinary Approaches to the Study of Mental Handicap published by ABA for the Royal Society of Medicine, UK.

Preface

Under the sponsorship of the Forum on Mental Retardation, The Royal Society of Medicine, a meeting was held at The University of Hull, UK, in 1987. The rather lengthy title of the programme, 'Social and environmental factors in the prevention and amelioration of mental handicap' accurately reflected its contents.

The multidisciplinary gathering of about forty professionals proved to be so profitable that it was subsequently decided to ask speakers to offer final versions of their lectures for publication. We acknowledge our debt to them, to the Royal Society of Medicine and to the University of Hull which provided an excellent milieu for one-and-a-half days of discussion.

The book itself offers an up-to-date coverage of the main research findings in the fields of prevention and amelioration of mental handicap. As such it includes epidemiology, primary prevention, secondary prevention and amelioration, education and educational and medical services. This overview outlines current challenges both to professionals in the field, and to society at large.

The meeting was chaired by the late Dr. David Morris who was the main instigator of the Forum on Mental Retardation and to whose memory this volume is dedicated. It is the first in a series to be published by ABA for the Forum on Mental Retardation on multidisciplinary approaches to the study of mental handicap.

Peter Evans
Alan Clarke

List of Main Contributors

Eva Alberman, M.D. Professor of Clinical Epidemiology, The London Hospital Medical College, The London Hospital, London E1 1BB.

Alfred A. Baumeister, Ph.D. Alexander Heard Distinguished Service Professor, Director, John F. Kennedy Center for Research on Education and Human Development, PO Box 40, Peabody College, Vanderbilt University, Nashville, Tennessee 37203.

Alan D. B. Clarke, C.B.E., Ph. D., D. Sc., C. PSYCHOL, F.B.Ps.S., HON F.R.C. PSYCH. Emeritus Professor, Department of Psychology, The University of Hull, Hull, HU6 7RX.

Tony Cline, B.Sc., C. PSYCHOL, Co-director for training in Educational Psychology, Department of Psychology, University College, London, Gower Street, London, WC1E 6BT.

Peter L. C. Evans, Ph. D., F.B.Ps.S., C. PSYCHOL. Senior Lecturer, Department of Educational Psychology and Special Educational Needs, The Institute of Education, University of London. Presently seconded to OECD, 2 Rue André Pascal, 75775 Paris, Cedex 16, France.

Thomas Fryers, Ph. D., M.D. Senior Lecturer, Department of Community Medicine, The University of Manchester, Manchester, M13 9PL.

Ronald Gulliford, C.B.E., Ph. D. Emeritus Professor, Department of Educational Psychology and Special Educational Needs, The University of Birmingham, Birmingham, B15 8AA.

Stephen A. Richardson, Ph. D. Professor Emeritus, Department of Pediatrics, Albert Einstein College of Medicine, Yeshiva University, 1300 Morris Park Avenue, New York 10461.

Michael Robertshaw, Cert.Ed. M.Sc Adv. Dip. Special Needs, Acting Director, Special Services, Leeds City Council, Department of Education, Selectapost 17, Merrion House, 110 Merrion Centre, Leeds LS2 8DT.

Euan Ross, M.D., F.R.C.P. Professor of Community Paediatrics and Honorary Consultant, Community Paediatrics, Kings College at St. Giles Hospital, London SE5 7RN..

Peter Sturmey, Ph.D., C. PSYCHOL. A.F.B.Ps., Senior Lecturer in Clinical Psychology, Department of Psychology, University of Birmingham, Birmingham, B15 8AA.

CHAPTER 1

Terminology and Concepts

Peter Evans

Department of Child Development and Educational Psychology, University of London Institute of Education, London

INTRODUCTION

Children and adults who are described as mentally handicapped represent a significant proportion of the population of any country. In general the term is taken to include those people who have IQs below 70/75 and who also show deficits in adaptive behaviour (e.g. Grossman, 1983). In children of school age, difficulties with educational progress will also be manifest and in England, at least, as many members of this group will find themselves in special schools. For those outside the age limits of compulsory education, i.e. 5-16, mentally handicapped pre-schoolers may be identified through failure to progress adequately through the developmental milestones and may start at state funded schools at the age of two. Those over 16 may remain in education for a further three years either at school or in college depending on the provision made by their LEA. Some may stay on to a later age in college on courses especially designed for vocational preparation and work. Those adults over the age of 19 who are still in need of the support of state agencies will continue to receive it through social service provision.

This book brings together a number of authors from the UK and the USA in medicine, psychology and education who have worked for many years with such children and adults and who are concerned from their various perspectives with the prevention and amelioration of mental handicap. Because any definition or conceptualisation of mental handicap must include some reference to the society in which that person lives and because our understanding of the problem has developed largely over the past 40 years, following major advances in social and medical science, several terminological systems have arisen and are used in the literature. They are also reflected in this book and discussed in detail in the chapter by Fryers. An overview of this issue is provided in the next section.

A NOTE ON TERMINOLOGY

Any scientific approach to understanding is ultimately concerned with establishing 'causes' and this is as true for workers in the field of mental handicap as it is for those in any other scientific area. It is from the identification of causes and their systematic description that a rational set of preventive programmes can be derived. As knowledge of mental handicap has progressed and the complexities of the problem have been unravelled, there have been changes in our understanding that have been so substantial that it has been thought necessary to introduce new descriptive terms and even to give them the force of law.

Since the 1950s there have been three major changes in England and Wales with parallel conceptual shifts in other countries, such as the USA, where different terminology is used. Thus in a short lifetime it has been necessary to come to grips with the scientific, but pejorative, terminology of feeble-minded, imbecile and idiot, through the concept of educational subnormality to the present terms of children with learning difficulties (1981, Education Act) which may be either severe or moderate. In the USA there has been a preference for the label mental retardation with sub-categories of educable, corresponding approximately with the word moderate, and trainable and profound with severe learning difficulty. The descriptor mental handicap is a generic one which tends to be used to refer to people who are outside of school age. It is also a common lay term. Mild mental handicap corresponds to educable mental retardation and moderate learning difficulty; severe mental handicap carries similar implications and corresponds to trainable and profound retardation to severe learning difficulty.

These changes in terminology are not purely gratuitous, but reflect adjustments in our understanding of the causes of mental handicap. These have moved from a model where the problems have been seen as residing within the child (e.g. as defined in the 1959 Mental Health Act) to one which gives more weight to the importance of environmental influences and the provision that any particular culture actually makes. These changes in understanding are reflected in legislation. There are two major events: a) the 1970 Education Act shifted the responsibility for the schooling of all mentally handicapped children from the medical to the educational authorities; and b) the 1981 Education Act abolished the categories referred to above as a means for making decisions about educational provision and replaced them with the concept of "special educational needs". This term is defined in that Act in the following way: "a child has 'special educational needs' if he has a learning difficulty which calls for special educational provision to be made for him". A

learning difficulty is defined as: "a)...a significantly greater difficulty in learning than the majority of children of his age; or b) ... a disability which either prevents or hinders him from making use of educational facilities of a kind generally provided in schools, within the area of the local authority concerned, for children of his age".
A third sub-clause provides a definition relating to pre- school children.

We are, then, saddled with sets of terms that vary from country to country, which have developed within a legislature, that serve different purposes and which reflect changes in the conceptualisation of the problem that have developed through research and practice. In addition, to some degree, the preferred term is also age related and workers from different backgrounds use the labels that suit them most and which seem most relevant to them. This is especially problematic in multi-disciplinary work involving educationalists and medical workers and the different terminologies in use are reflected in this book. The matter is further complicated by the inclusion of several chapters by authors from the USA.

It has been recognised for many years that, from a scientific point of view, these administrative concepts are of little value in defining groups for comparative purposes. What of course is required are more precise identifiers that are related to the scientific questions that are being studied. The establishment of groups consisting of people with identifiable chromosomal abnormalities, is one such way if the investigation is concerned with identifying, for example, the causes of their development. The outcome of such research might well have practical preventive consequences. Alternatively, groups might be determined on the basis of a typology derived from an understanding of the learning process (e.g. Evans,1982). The outcome of this approach might well have implications for the planning of individualised educational interventions with a more ameliorative goal in mind. Nevertheless the terms severe learning difficulty (SLD) and moderate learning difficulty (MLD) are frequently used in their administrative context, and often, but incorrectly, given aetiological significance, usually based on the widely held view that the causes of SLD are different from those of MLD. The central problem is that while it may well be a useful generalisation to claim that certain pathological conditions may be highly correlated with severe learning difficulty, or with children with IQs of less than 50, and cultural-familial factors with moderate learning difficulty, or with children with IQs between 50 and 70, it may not be assumed that children in schools described as being for either severe or moderate learning difficulty neatly fit this theoretical description. Furthermore, the use of the IQ in defining such groups is also of limited value since we know that scores on such tests may be highly influenced by unusual environmental factors, e.g. Clarke and Clarke (1976).

The work of the Hagbergs, in Sweden, may be used to illustrate some of the points referred to above (e.g. Hagberg and Hagberg, 1984); (but see Fryers, this volume). Using the IQ descriptors of SLD and MLD given above they claimed that 81% of SLD children in contrast to 43% of MLD children had an identifiable biological cause that could be traced to a number of pre-, peri-, and postnatal influences. Their breakdown is given in Table 1.

TABLE 1
Table showing pre-, peri- and postnatal origins of mental retardation found in Gothenburg, Sweden. (Adapted from Hagberg and Hagberg, 1984).

		SLD (%)	MLD (%)
Prenatal		55	23
Perinatal		15	18
Postnatal		11	2
		—	—
	Total	81	43

In addition to the aetiologies identified in Table 1, with regard to the MLD group, and maintaining the IQ definition, we would need to add those children with low IQs, related to cultural-familial factors, which involve an interaction between genetic and environmental influences, and which may or may not come to be reported. The main problem here is that one of the principal ways in which such children come to be identified is through failure at school. If such difficulties are associated with behaviour problems these children are more likely to be identified than those with milder manners who may well pass unnoticed, thus biasing the sample. The value of the IQ score in attempting to identify those with genuinely low ability is problematic since, as already indicated, scores on these tests may be artificially depressed by adverse environmental factors and in any event if they are to be taken to reflect inherited ability it is necessary to assume that the individuals making up the group have had optimal educational experiences (Clarke and Clarke, 1976) and thus will be giving of their best during testing— a highly dubious assumption indeed.

It is for the sorts of reasons discussed above that many workers particularly in educational settings have come to feel that a clear distinction between SLD, MLD and other children showing slow progress is no longer either tenable or useful. They are much happier with the idea of a continuum of special educational needs (SEN) which is related to available provision (see Evans, 1988 for one such model). However, at the same time it must not be forgotten that there are pathological conditions and biologically rooted causes of mental handicap that will provide a completely different descriptive framework and which serve to operate with different purposes in mind. Moreover, multifactorial influences may operate in the individual case.

Thus we are dealing with a highly complex issue, the subtleties of which will become apparent to the reader who progresses through this book. However, it is hoped that the discussion given above will help to contextualise some of the matters raised in this collection concerned with the prevention and amelioration of mental handicap from the various perspectives on offer.

PRIMARY PREVENTION AND AMELIORATION

Primary prevention. Primary prevention refers to the rather strict criterion of the prevention of the initiation of conditions that are known to be strongly predictive of retardation. It is worth noting that under this definition terminations of pregnancies where e.g. Down's Syndrome is indicated are not examples of primary prevention since a fetus displaying an abnormal chromosomal pattern has already been created. Note too, however, that conceptually this idea is much easier to grasp if one works within a purely biological referent. That is, it is assumed that chromosomal disorders lead to conditions which are so closed to amelioration that people with such abnormalities will necessarily become mentally handicapped, with the implication that they will show deficits in adaptive behaviour. This must be seen as a contentious assumption which raises practical, social and ethical questions which are not resolvable through arguments based solely on genetic principles. This is because deficits in adaptive behaviour are not absolute characteristics but are determined in relation to a society's own customs and levels of tolerance. Nevertheless, in the prevailing social climate many of these circumstances do lead to pathological conditions, which the majority of people would wish to prevent if at all possible; viz the take-up of amniocentesis by women in the most critical age range.

Primary prevention in SLD. Many of the advances in medical science in this area relate to the identification of biological causes. Alberman discusses the principal developments in true primary prevention in her chapter which focusses on primary prevention of SLD. She includes a discussion of the prevention of neural-tube defects through dietary supplement and genetic counselling before conception. Finally those forms of primary prevention that can occur after birth are noted. These include the prevention of accidents, non-accidental injury, the infection of the brain and/or its membranes and the new advances in the effective treatment of brain tumours. These forms of primary prevention are also, of course, related to increases in the social and material circumstances of the citizenry.

In addition Alberman discusses preventive methods, that are not strictly primary, which occur after conception but before birth and which allow for the detection of abnormalities using techniques such as the monitoring of alpha-fetoprotein, amniocentesis and chorionic villus biopsy. The last method may be especially useful in cases where a further pregnancy follows a previously affected fetus, for example, in the case of one of the mucopolysaccharide diseases.

There are many other methods that also exist and which are well tested in the area of primary prevention. Immunisation for rubella is one well known example. Others include the prevention of maternal access to teratogenic agents such as some antibiotics, of prenatal infections, of rhesus factors and the complex balance between the prevention of damage in the case of premature births and the maintenance of life in the face of likely incomplete development in a hospital's intensive care facility.

Primary prevention in MLD. Primary prevention for those children said to have moderate learning difficulties is an equally complex problem to that described above for SLD as the various chapters of this book indicate. Following the 1981 Education Act children with MLD are technically those with "statements" under that Act indicating that they are in need of a modified curriculum. This may be put into practice in either special or mainstream schools, but it must be admitted that it is a rather vague notion. Nevertheless it seems to be the case that many such children come from a variety of backgrounds that are underprivileged and from families who do not meet the usually accepted social norms. For these children the principal method of primary prevention has to lie in the reduction of these adverse circumstances and the development of appropriate attitudes to child rearing in order to promote physical and mental health. As the situation stands at present, however, most of the work has to be carried out at the levels of secondary prevention and amelioration.

SECONDARY PREVENTION AND AMELIORATION

Secondary Prevention. Secondary prevention aims to overcome already existing or developing handicaps. For children who potentially may develop SLD, where the aetiology is well known, clear examples of secondary prevention may be cited. For instance, damage to the brain, due to the toxic effects of incompletely broken down metabolic products as in phenylketonuria (PKU), may be considerably reduced by dietary control, serves as one such well documented example. However, once a clear aetiology ceases to be discernible and once a more transactional understanding of the social nature of mental handicap, particularly for those with moderate conditions, becomes more understood and accepted then concepts such as secondary prevention become rather less clear. For example some discussions of secondary prevention (e.g. Schwartz and Johnson, 1985) include early stimulation programmes with children considered to be 'at risk' who had not been identified as MLD. Clearly if the programmes work well then the potential MLD children who have been involved and who do not turn out to require special educational services surely may be said to have received primary prevention- i.e. without such early stimulation they would have been found to have been in need of such services: (see for example the discussion of the long-term effects of early education programmes by Lazar and Darlington, 1982). For those particular children to have been involved in a secondary prevention programme one would have had to have known in advance that they had an extant handicap. Thus because many handicaps, especially in the moderate condition, are likely to be largely socially determined it is not always clear whether one is is describing primary or secondary prevention.

Amelioration. For most children who are experiencing severe or moderate learning difficulties the best that can be done is to work on systems intended to ameliorate these conditions and to prevent additional problems from arising. This requires a broad approach and the majority of the chapters in this book are concerned with aspects of this work. These extend from the organisation of preschool parental involvement programmes and the delivery of school based and adult systems and services, both educational and medical, to an analysis of professionals' perceptions of the new term MLD. The educational aspects in particular are put into an historical context.

CONCLUSIONS

Mental handicap is a challenging area. There have been many advances over the years both in medical and social science that have been aimed at preventing and ameliorating suffering for both individuals and families alike, but the complexities must not be underestimated. With time, it has become increasingly clear that total intervention can only ever come about through the combined efforts of workers in various fields of activity. It is hoped that the collection of chapters offered in this book will aid that multi-disciplinary goal through the increased mutual understanding of the various assumptions and practices of the others' discipline.

REFERENCES

Clarke, A.M. & Clarke, A.D.B. (1976) Overview and implications. In A.M. Clarke and A.D.B. Clarke (Eds.) *Early Experience: Myth and Evidence.* London: Open Books.

Education Act (1971) London: HMSO.

Education Act (1981) London: HMSO.

Evans, P. L. C. (1982) Inhibition and individual differences in inhibitory processes in retarded children. In N.R. Ellis (Ed.) *International Review of Research in Mental Retardation,* **11,** *80-123.*

Evans, P. L. C. (1988) Towards a social psychology of special education. *Educational and Child Psychology,* **5.** 7.8.90.

Grossman, H. J. (Ed.) (1983) *Classification in Mental Retardation.* Washington, DC: American Association on Mental Deficiency.

Hagberg, B. & Hagberg, G. (1984) Aspects of prevention of pre- peri- and postnatal brain pathology in severe and mild mental retardation. In J. Dobbing, A. D.B. Clarke, J. A. Corbett, J. Hogg, and R. O. Robinson (Eds.) *Scientific Studies in Mental Retardation.* London: Royal Society of Medicine and MacMillan.

Lazar, I.. & Darlington, R. B. (1982) Lasting effects of early education. *Monographs of the Society for Research in Child Development,* **47**, 1-141.

Mental Health Act (1959) London: HMSO.

Schwartz, S. & Johnson, J. H. (1985) *Psychopathology of Childhood.* Oxford: Pergamon Press.

CHAPTER 2

Epidemiology of Severe Mental Retardation

Tom Fryers

Department of Community Medicine, University of Manchester, UK

INTRODUCTION

Mental retardation poses many problems for epidemiologists, not least in the fundamental issues of definition, measurement, and classification. These problems are not new, but they have not always been recognised in the past. Terms have proliferated (Figure 1), representing groups ill-defined or not defined at all, and implying vague and often unacknowledged concepts. These latter have always encompassed 'low intelligence', learning difficulties, and inadequate social adaptation, but description, definition, measurement, and classification of these terms have been contentious. Medical writers have tended to imply some underlying 'biological' coherence in the grouping, without ever being able to define its nature.

	Defect	
Mental	Subnormality	Profound
Intellectual	Handicap	Severe
Learning	Retardation	Moderate
Developmental	Impairment	Mild
	Disability	Border-line

(Any combination may be tried: most are already in use somewhere!)

Figure 1
Terms currently employed

When we had little knowledge of organic causes of central nervous system impairment, and could discriminate only crudely between clinical types, it seemed proper to study the group as a whole, and try to differentiate the 'causes' of different degrees of low intelligence, classically simplified into 'organic' causes of severe retardation and 'social' or 'cultural' causes of mild retardation. The facts, such as they were, never really fitted any classification, and as knowledge of organic aetiologies associated with low intelligence has increased it has become increasingly difficult to justify treating 'mental retardation' as an epidemiological entity. This was foreseen by O'Connor in 1965, when he wrote "The possibility of judging prevalence in a syndrome such as mental deficiency might very well be discarded as a mistaken idea, resulting from a confusion of many separate entities, each given the blanket title of mental defect".

Arguments continue, however, about the general term to be preferred and its definition, but the debate is very confused. First, there is often no discrimination between, on the one hand, the need for terms in general use in society, which must be socially acceptable to clients, parents and workers, and on the other, the requirement for terms precisely defined for research use. Rarely can the criteria arising from these two extremely disparate needs be the same, so we must accept different usages for different contexts. This chapter is concerned exclusively with a research context. Secondly, the search for one all- embracing definition to suit all needs, often implied by the nature of the arguments, is spurious. There is no need to have only one definition, or set of definitions; indeed, there is great potential in a variety of definitions to suit different purposes.

A TAXONOMY OF DEFINITIONS RELATED TO MENTAL RETARDATION

The WHO classification of impairments, disabilities and handicaps (WHO, 1980; Wood and Badley, 1978), provides a useful structure for definitions related to mental retardation.

Global:	Intellectual Impairment. Learning Disability. Mental Handicap/Retardation. (Developmental Handicap?) (Retardation Handicap?) (Services)
Partial:	Aetiological entities — specific impairments. Specific disabilities and syndromes. Specific handicaps — including families. Associated impairments, disabilities, diseases and behaviours. (Services)

Figure 2
Concepts and Definitions

Figure 2 shows the various *different* definitions which can be used for epidemiological investigation according to the purpose to be served (Fryers, 1987; 1988) There are 'global' definitions, describing the group as a whole, and 'partial' definitions, which are not *exclusively* related to mental retardation.

Global Categories

Intellectual Impairment implies a conception of 'intellect' as analogous to a body system (such as an enzyme system) representing the central nervous system's capacity to learn, and impairment is the appropriate term in the WHO classification. This definition will be used if we wish to study groups defined by *intelligence.* It is measured by intelligence tests, the advantages and disadvantages, problems and merits of which, can be studied and debated scientifically (Berger and Yule, 1985). Similarly, in populations, problems of standardization for particular populations, and changes in population means are susceptible to scientific investigation.

*Learning Disability** describes groups defined in terms of learning difficulty, measured by educational instruments such as reading tests. Where education is universal, it is likely to incorporate all severely intellectually impaired children, some mildly intellectually impaired children, and some whose learning difficulties are not related to intellectual impairment. If it seems less applicable to adults except by reference to earlier school experience, this is only because we do not often give educational tests to adults. Exceptions might include army recruits and prison populations, where non-readers accumulate (Roberts, 1986).

'Handicap' is personal and social disadvantage, and *Mental Handicap* relates this to 'mental' problems; 'mental' is a wholly unsatisfactory word, but no one has produced a more appropriate one. Its use also for mental illness, which may also be disabling and handicapping, is necessarily confusing, since we have long been at pains to stress the distinctions between the two groups. Retardation is a term with more explicit meaning, but has been used more as a synonym for 'handicap' in this context. Perhaps the most logical and useful term would be *Retardation Handicap,* but it seems unlikely that this could now be established in professional use! *Developmental Handicap*

* In some parts of the world, e.g. the USA, this term implies a discrepancy of about 1 standard deviation between a score derived from an IQ test and a lower score derived from an educational test.

might be more readily accepted; it carries the implication of interference in *childhood* development which is the almost universal convention, but it could logically include those with physical maldevelopment but normal intelligence. We probably have to accept that current usage equates mental handicap and mental retardation, that both imply an association with relatively low intelligence and with learning difficulties, but neither implies a limitation to *particular* degrees of intellectual impairment or types of learning disability.

What is most important to recognise is that, though it will encompass many individuals with organic brain disorder, mental handicap is a *socially* defined group. It varies very widely between different societies (see Richardson and Koller, 1985) because of different legal, administrative and professional processes, together with their underlying policies, traditions, attitudes, and perceptions which determine selection as mentally handicapped. Selection is more likely in the presence of motor and sensory disabilities, abnormal behaviour, and effects of deprivation. But without comprehensive social explanations, prevalence statistics for the group as a whole are of little value except to inform local service managers of the totality of their clients.

Accepting the convention of IQ <50 for *severe intellectual impairment*, all individuals within this group will necessarily have learning disability, and will almost invariably be incorporated into socially defined mental handicap or retardation. If operational definitions of *severe* learning disability and *severe* mental handicap are restricted to people with IQ <50, as they often are, then these groups will be identical and co-terminus. In this case IQ <50 becomes the sole necessary criterion for them all, and this has given some, limited consistency to definitions used for studies of the severe group over the last 30 years.

Conversely, operational definitions of mild learning disability and mild mental handicap/retardation, never include all those of IQ 50-69, the conventional definition of mild intellectual impairment. They sometimes include people of high ability. These (mild) groups are never identical or co-terminus, and the relative independence of mild mental retardation from intellectual impairment creates a conceptual discontinuity with severe retardation. Researchers have despaired of finding a basis for comparison in mild or total retardation categories, generally looking to organic features, but scientific comparison is both possible and needed, to examine the *determinants of selection* in different societies. In this, as so often, epidemiology and other social sciences must work together (Mercer, 1965; 1970).

Generalisations about the epidemiology of *severe* mental retardation, co-terminus with severe intellectual impairment, do have some validity, though it seems likely that, as professional interest and service engagement continue to expand and diversify, there will be less and less consistency of operational definition in the future. It is possible that studies of severe retardation will be soon redundant or inappropriate. However, accepting it for what it has been, it is worthwhile reviewing the outlines of current knowledge, which, from experience, is not widely understood, and some of the questions raised by current ignorance in the light of epidemiological studies of three decades.

SEVERE INTELLECTUAL IMPAIRMENT: SEVERE MENTAL RETARDATION

The use of incidence* statistics of mental retardation is not very helpful because of the many different types of disorder, resulting from many different agents and processes operating from before conception through to adulthood. Prevalence in human populations is dynamic in response both to variations in incidence, and to variations in mortality (Fryers, 1984) and varies in the following not unconnected ways.

1) There is geographical variation between different communities at the same time, in particular age groups: for example, in the last 30 years in developed countries, reliable studies of relatively small (5 year) child age groups have varied from 1.62/1000 for children aged 5-9 years, born 1951-55, in Salford CB (Kushlick, 1961), to 7.34/1000 for children aged 13 years, born 1957 in Amsterdam (Sorel, 1974). There are very many factors which we would expect to influence these figures differentially in different communities, but communities of similar genetic stock, culture, vital statistics, economic and social conditions, and health and related service provision, might expect similar patterns of prevalence at the same time. Communities which differ in these characteristics will expect to differ in prevalence of severe M.R. at any particular age: this is particularly true of developing countries in general. (Fryers, 1984; 1986a; Diaz-Fernandez amd Gestal-Otero, 1987).

2) Differential migration is an important factor in determining prevalence ratios in particular communities, for particular age and sex groups, and at particular times. For example, where significant numbers of mentally retarded people are in long-term residential care, their experience of migration will be different from that of the

* Readers unfamiliar with the terms incidence and prevalence may wish for definitions; Incidence refers to the number of cases arising in a population whereas prevalence relates to the total number of cases within an age group or total population

general population. If the population has diminished, prevalence ratios will tend to be high; if the population has increased, ratios will tend to be low. Similarly, if a significant proportion of young adults leaves a community for further education, work or marriage, prevalence ratios for disabled people in that age group will be inflated by the reduced denominator (Der and Wooff, 1986).

3) There is variation between birth cohorts in the same community. For example, prevalence in the age group 5-09 years in Salford CB, varied from 1.98/1000 in 1961, to 5.54/1000 in 1971, then to 3.86/1000 in 1961, to 5.54/1000 in 1971, then to 2.86/1000 in 1980. Some of this is due to variation in incidence of particular aetiological groups; some of it changes in mortality before, during and after birth; some may be due to changes in some aspects of ascertainment.

4) There is a consistent pattern of variation over time throughout the developed world - the range of reliable figures for 5 year cohorts of school age children, was approximately 1.5 - 4.0/1000 for those born in the early 1970s; and has been falling ever since. The increase was almost certainly the result of increasing survival from birth and infancy in that period; the decrease seems to be the result of many different processes by which the incidence of several specific organic causes has fallen (Fryers, 1984). There is also the possibility of some children making gains in performance from earlier education which removes them from the 'severe' group, but this shift over the border is likely to be very small.

5) There are great and changing variations in prevalence between age groups in any one community, because of cohort variations in the incidence of specific causes, and relatively high but decreasing mortality at all ages (as well as any effects of migration). Reasonable estimates of prevalence of severe mental handicap in an 'average' English Health District with a stable population, for the second half of the 1980s would be as in Table 1.

If any community has special features which might affect the incidence of particular conditions, (such as many older mothers producing more Down's syndrome babies, or a large ethnic group with high obstetric risks) or survival, (such as a high infant mortality, or an epidemic affecting a particular cohort of children), then these figures might be substantially varied. In every community they will vary over time because of cohort variations: they will not be the same in 10 years!

6) Recent prevalence figures for older age groups suggest considerable increases in most developed communities, with increased survival of all age groups. Recent figures include: 3.53/1000 aged 35-54 years, in Ireland, in 1981 (Mulcahy et al., 1983); 2.08/1000 aged 50-59 years, in Bristol, in 1980 (Russell and Hall, 1980); 1.96/1000 aged 55-54 years, in Salford MD, in1982. The mean age at

TABLE 1

Current Estimates of Age-specific Prevalence of Severe Retardation in an Average English District of Stable Population

Age	0 — 4:	2.5/1000
	5 — 9:	3.0/1000
	10—14:	4.0/1000
	15—19:	4.5/1000
	20—24:	5.0/1000
	25—34:	4.0/1000
	35—44:	3.0/1000
	45—54:	2.5/1000
	55—64:	2.0/1000
	65—74:	1.0/1000
	75+:	very few

death appears to be moving steadily towards the normal population, (Carter and Jancar, 1983). Very much increased survival at all ages is well documented for Down's Syndrome (Stein and Susser, 1975; Fryers, 1986b), and we can reasonably assume that it applies to other groups, though probably to varying degrees.

7) The sex ratio in prevalence studies usually slightly favours males, but there is little evidence of any general pattern from prevalence studies, except a hint that there may be an increasing sex ratio with increasing prevalence due to increasing survival (Fryers, 1984; Richardson, 1987).

8) The 'social class' distribution of severe retardation has usually been considered to be equal across all classes, a very surprising feature when social determinants are so significant in almost all other health problems. It is likely that a social class gradient in incidence has been masked by a similar gradient in early mortality, but this is probably changing with increases in survival. However, 'social class' data are very difficult to interpret between different cultures and times, and future studies will need great sociological sophistication if they are to elucidate the issue (Fryers, 1984).

Partial Categories

Aetiology: Agents, Factors, and Processes

'Cause' is a complex and subtle concept and must be related to precise definitions. It is almost always multi-factorial and is best considered in dynamic terms, as a process. Even for an organic pathology of known origin, many other factors, known or unknown, have usually contributed to the ultimate outcome, especially if the outcome is the disabilities and handicaps experienced by a human individual. The impairments of rubella syndrome are the result of foetal infection: but what determines the particular configuration of impairments; what determines foetal infection after maternal infection; and what determines maternal infection? The factors and processes causing damage to brain cells and connections are enigmatic; those causing diminished intelligence are mysterious. Where there is no evidence of organic disorder, the 'causes' of low intelligence must be conceived in terms of polygenic inheritance and its interaction with specific environments in a particular family and cultural context (Clarke, 1985).

These questions are most pertinent to intellectual impairment. For learning disability and mental handicap, other factors unrelated to intellectual impairment, such as sensory loss or behaviour disorder, also affect designation. Other environmental influences also determine selection: common perceptions and prejudices, professional assumptions and practices, service structures and resources, and so on. We cannot talk of 'cause' in relation to mental retardation without encompassing organic, psychological and social processes.

Nevertheless, with regard to *severe* retardation, organic processes are of paramount importance, since serious disorder of the central nervous system usually has devastating effects on intelligence, physical development, and behaviour, and may legitimately be considered the principal cause of the syndrome and its consequences for the individual. Studies have demonstrated brain pathology in all people designated *severely* retarded, but few organic syndromes, pathologies or causal processes are exclusive to *severe* retardation. Most also contribute to mild retardation and almost certainly to reduced intelligence in people of higher ability.

For this reason, retardation is not the best starting point for investigation, and the proportions of organic syndromes within retardation categories are not very useful statistics, though commonly published. If epidemiology is to inform preventive and ameliorative intervention, we should rather study the spectrum of impairments, disabilities, and handicaps displayed within each aetiological category, and follow up cohorts to observe natural history in terms of measured intelligence, disabilities and handicaps throughout life. There have as yet been few such studies. Most disorders are extremely rare, and need vast populations for study, not limited to retardation. We have insecure frequency data for most, which do not yet provide a base line for evaluating preventive intervention. This is illustrated later with reference to fragile X.

THE CONTRIBUTION OF SPECIFIC ORGANIC DISORDERS TO SEVERE MENTAL RETARDATION

1. A confident diagnosis with aetiological implications can be given in most cases of severe retardation where full examination is possible. It is disputed whether the proportion known is of the order of 80-90% or only 50-60%, but this depends largely upon what is accepted as a 'known' cause. Sometimes we have a fairly complete understanding of the basic aetiology such as rubella syndrome, or measles encephalitis. Sometimes we know a great deal about the mechanism of causation, but little of causative agents, as in Down's syndrome where the ultimate causes of non- dysjunction are quite unknown. Sometimes we know of causative agents but not much of processes, as with anoxic or hypoglycaemic birth injury. Sometimes we acknowledge a precise genetic aetiology, but cannot say why some individuals are intellectually impaired and others not, as with tuberose sclerosis. Some clearly identifiable syndromes can be recognised but we know little yet of agents or processes. If all are included, the proportion 'known' probably exceeds 80%. Currently by no means all these are susceptible to preventive intervention, but in most there are clear directions for further research. It is not necessary to know the whole of the aetiological story to be able to intervene, and hope is strong in many cases.

2. Although all severely retarded people have neurological impairments with organic, often genetic causes, many factors known to determine the incidence of specific aetiologies are, nevertheless, 'social' and many reflect aspects of the health care system (see Fryers, 1986a). Down's syndrome varies with maternal age distribution, patterns of marriage, family size, contraceptive use, availability and acceptability of deliberate abortion, and so on. Recessive microcephaly may only be commonly found where consanguinous marriages are the cultural norm, and not easily changed; Tay Sachs disease, similarly recessively inherited in Ashkenazi communities, depends upon the acceptability of pre-marital genetic counselling, if offered. Congenital syphilis varies with levels of prostitution, general patterns of sexual behaviour, and fear of AIDS, as well as access to early treatment.

Fetal alcohol syndrome - claimed and disputed recently as the 'largest cause of mental retardation' (Abel and Sokol, 1986; Livingstone and Lyall, 1986) (but how defined, and of what degree?!), must vary with patterns of consumption, government alcohol policies, levels of unemployment, and health education offered to young women, amongst many other factors. Rubella syndrome depends, inter alia, upon herd immunity, the effectiveness of immunisation programmes, and current myths about vaccine risks. Perinatal damage depends in part upon the quality of ante-natal and intra-natal care, in part upon maternal nutrition, and, possibly, attitudes to care. Mental retardation due to congenital hypo-thyroidism varies with environmental iodine deficiency, and depends upon the comprehensiveness of iodine supplementation in endemic areas, and neonatal screening in all areas. This latter also applies to the inherited disorders of metabolism.

These factors and many others may shift the incidence of particular disorders, but inexplicable changes also occur, such as recent reductions in neural tube defects (Leck, 1983a). In addition each particular disorder may vary in incidence by sex, social class, race, and other personal or environmental factors.

3. The prevalence of each disorder is influenced not only by incidence and factors affecting incidence, but also by mortality and factors affecting mortality. Thus prevalence at birth of Down's syndrome is as dependent upon fetal loss, natural and un- natural, as upon incidence of Down's conceptuses. Since precise knowledge of natural foetal loss is hard to come by, though recent work suggests that it is very high, we cannot yet be sure of prevalence at conception (Roman and Stevenson, 1983; Maclean, 1987). Lower peri-natal mortality has almost certainly been accompanied by more impaired children surviving birth. Similarly increased survival at all ages, clearly demonstrated for Down's syndrome (Stein and Susser, 1975; Leck, 1983b; Fryers, 1986b), probably applies variably to all other aetiological categories too.

Both the varying incidence and the varying mortality of these many disorders will affect the prevalence of the group as a whole; for this reason we should expect the prevalence of severe mental retardation, however carefully defined, to vary from place to place and time to time.

4. Mental retardation is particularly characterised by the great multiplicity and diversity of the aetiological entities which contribute to it. Since both incidence and prevalence of most groups are variable, their proportional contributions to severe retardation as a whole (even assuming consistency of definition of the whole group) must vary too. Moreover, as already emphasised, many disorders contribute also to mild retardation and to the population without intellectual impairment. This renders proportional morbidity statistics within even severe mental retardation, of little value. If Down's syndrome diminishes as older women have fewer babies, its contribution to severe retardation will diminish, and the percentage of all other causal categories will increase. Such mutually dependent figures are neither helpful nor necessary: in communities where good prevalence statistics are obtained, there will also be good

population statistics, and there is little excuse for not expressing each causal category in terms of population frequency.

The problem is multiplied when figures are derived from hospital samples of unknown relationship to the general population. Such figures are of little value or interest. Where they can be related precisely to a base population, they should be expressed as population rates and ratios, when they might indicate minimum frequencies. Statistics for aetiological groups derived from all people identified as retarded in a known population are likely to provide better indications of minimal frequencies, but only representative samples from total populations will provide the reliable population incidence and prevalence figures we need, to clarify the relationship between intellectual impairment and a particular disorder and to inform preventive intervention.

This can be illustrated by recent published work on 'fragile X syndrome'. Froster-Iskenius (1983) reported 6.2% and other similar proportions of institutionalised mentally retarded men. This showed that the disorder exists in such groups, and is not negligible But how can such selected samples be compared, or related to base populations? Jacobs et al. (1983) reported 1.8% of a 'non representative' community sample, which raises the same questions. Blomquist et al. (1982, 1983) reported 6% of all severely retarded boys in their population: if expressed as population ratios, this might indicate minimum prevalence, assuming a positive association between fragile X, intellectual impairment, and mental retardation. Webb et al. (1986), reported frequencies of 73/100,000 (1/1362) boys and 61/100,000 (1/1630) girls in Coventry special schools, and Turner et al. (1986) reported fragile X associated with retardation (but how defined and measured?) of 38/100,000 (1/2610) boys and 24/100,000 (1/4221) girls in Australian state schools.

By this time some epidemiological light was beginning to fall on the situation, and the Lancet leader of November 22nd 1986 suggested an overall prevalence of about 1/1000 at age 11-16. Other work has suggested that as many as 80% of males with the fragile site show retardation (but how defined and measured?), but this is true of only about 30% of females. The other 70% are carriers, with a 1/2 risk of male children being retarded and 1/6 risk for female children (Evans and Hamerton, 1985). The latest studies raise the possibilities of screening and genetic counselling, because sound epidemiological studies have at last established whole population frequencies and the relationship of the gene anomaly to clinical states and carrier status.

Do we know the 'cause', and its consequences in individuals and populations, or only part of the process of causation, and some associations in populations? There is much more precision and detail to be worked out, particularly to clarify the relationship of fragile X to different degrees of intellectual impairment in whole populations. There is still the process by which the gene anomaly produces intellectual and somatic impairments to be elucidated, and reasons established why some individuals are affected more than others. Any part of the complex process resulting in diminished intelligence might open up possibilities of preventive intervention. But a start has been made and rapid advances are currently expected in this field.

5. Evidence of cause and effect may be difficult to demonstrate with such low frequencies in populations. For example, no one doubts that asphyxia during birth can cause serious neurological and intellectual impairment. Most recent attention has focussed on low birth weight babies. Studies tend to show, as one would expect, higher frequencies of low intelligence in later life, particularly in babies very light for gestational age (Illsley and Mitchell, 1984; McCormick, 1985). But the proportion of children with significant disabilities seems to have diminished as obstetric and paediatric techniques have improved, and the same interventions which save the lives of very small babies, some damaged, are likely to prevent damage in larger babies, previously at high risk. The end product of this dynamic equation in any population is impossible to estimate. For this reason, because of very small numbers now involved, and because of the immense difficulty in defining and measuring the precise input factors in asphyxia, and the precise outcome in neurological and intellectual terms, I believe this is not now capable of solution by traditional epidemiological approaches. Concentrating on factors associated with low birth weight per se may be more fruitful.

Specific Disabilities and Disability Syndromes Associated With Severe Mental Retardation

Understanding aetiological processes is supremely important for prevention. Structural impairments may rarely be ameliorable by surgery and in the future transplant and gene manipulation techniques may have potential for 'curative' intervention, but for most disabled children and adults, it is the ensuing disabilities which have the greatest and most conscious impact on their lives, limit their potential, and render them variously dependent on others. Specific disabilities commonly affect moving, seeing, hearing, speaking, communicating and relating to others, and none is exclusive to retardation.

In respect of cerebral palsy, Jarvis and Hey (1984) commented: "it is surprising that so little has been done to measure objectively the disability and handicap caused by these disorders". The same applies to mental retardation: study of the frequency, associations, and natural history of disabilities may inform secondary and tertiary prevention and its evaluation, but it is only recently that clearly thought out work has been much attempted. In the future studies might usefully combine retarded and non-retarded populations.

A classic use of epidemiology is the identification of syndromes; groups of signs and symptoms which are commonly found together, and which may therefore constitute an aetiological, pathological, or therapeutic entity. Epidemiological studies have identified, confirmed and clarified the 'pervasive developmental disabilities' (autism) and the 'triad of social and language impairments' in recent years (Wing and Gould, 1979). This work identifies a group of children with common special needs, but also provokes important questions about pathology and aetiology.

Wing has also developed a standardised research instrument for the epidemiological study of disabilities, (HBS schedule: Wing and Gould, 1978) which has been used in several countries (Cooper, 1981). The interaction of many measurable characteristics in a mentally retarded population has been explored in Mannheim (Cooper et al., 1987). Five groups of children were identified by particular patterns of disability, deemed more valid in reflecting problems and needs than psychometric test performance alone. In particular, one group (about 1/1000 children of school age) seemed to be predominantly handicapped by disabilities of behaviour and social interaction, requiring specific remedial intervention. These groups also offer new opportunities for research into causal agents and processes.

A short survey instrument, (Disability Assessment Schedule, DAS) has been derived from the HBS schedule, and used for evaluating re-location of hospitalised populations, and population studies of disabilities in severely retarded people. Apart from the basic epidemiological interest - eg in the clustering of disabilities - it has planning application in identifying staff skills required in a community based service. This approach also offers the possibility of evaluating new service arrangements by monitoring the disabilities exhibited by a whole client group.

Specific Handicaps Associated with Severe Retardation

Specific Handicaps have also been little studied, though the disadvantages which accrue to individuals, families and groups related to retardation, are many, varied, and serious. They include financial hardship, exclusion from generic services, employment problems, social stigma, and many others. A few have focused on these, though usually concentrating on mildly retarded people (e.g. Richardson, 1978; 1980), and the service evaluation studies from Sheffield encompassed elements of handicap (Heron and Myers, 1983). Amongst the most important handicaps for study are those affecting parents and families; there have been a few studies of parental and family burdens (e.g. Wilkin, 1979; 1981; Dupont, 1980; Carr, 1985). Much more is needed.

As with aetiological entities and specific disabilities, such handicaps are not restricted to those with intellectual impairment. Research broader in scope could prove helpful in promoting action if those with, for example financial hardship due to inadequate welfare benefits, made common cause with all suffering the handicap.

Associated Impairments, Disabilities, Diseases, and Behaviours

Severe intellectual impairment in populations is associated with very high frequencies of somatic impairments, motor and sensory disabilities, psychiatric illness, and challenging behaviours.

Some are part of the syndrome related to the aetiology, such as rubella syndrome; some are concurrent high frequencies such as congenital anomalies; some are common in specific disorders, such as congenital heart defects in Down's people; some are secondary to the original disorder, such as self inflicted injury; some are incidental. They need to be recognised clinically and epidemiologically as independent entities as well as in relationship to intellectual impairment. For many individuals, these features constitute the greatest source of disablement. They often mask the true extent of learning potential, and make testing difficult, but may also offer the greatest hope for significant amelioration.

Thus the overlaps with epilepsy, cerebral palsy, sensory loss, and psychiatric disorder, are particularly important. Epidemiological study of these phenomena has increased considerably in recent years, but all pose methodological and practical problems. Accepting the insecurity of denominators, between 20 and 50% of severely retarded people may have epilepsy, but studies do not usually clarify how many are controlled (Cooper and Ort, 1983; Corbett, 1981). The approach of Cavazutti et al. (1984), may prove more useful, following up infants with various types of seizure experience. Various figures, mostly 20-40%, have been quoted for cerebral palsy in severely retarded populations (Corbett, 1981). Reliable figures for prevalence of auditory and visual impairments are even harder to find. There are major problems of definition and measurement for all these, but better prognosis and understanding of causal factors susceptible to intervention are more likely to come from studies of whole populations not specifically related to retardation (Neugebauer and Susser, 1979; Stanley and Alberman, 1984; Kiely, 1984).

Psychiatric illness is somewhat different in that psychiatrists have claimed very varied frequencies related to severe retardation, but few are clearly defined illness categories as applied to the rest of the population. This is understandable given the problems of communication, performance and behaviour inherent in the examination of severely retarded people. Everything depends upon definition, diagnosis and classification, a complex and contentious issue in itself (Corbett, 1985). Two recent surveys from Sweden reported 64% and 71% of severely retarded children and adults respectively, with 'major psychiatric disorder' (Gillberg et al., 1986; Gostason and Akesson, 1986), but the latter found no excess of schizophrenia or affective psychosis compared to the rest of the population. The situation was reviewed in 1979 by James and Snaith. In older age groups, there is evidence of much higher frequencies of dementia of the Alzheimer type in severely retarded adults, particularly in Down's people, for whom it has been suggested that from 50 to 100% of those over 40 show recognizable signs (Lubin and Kiely, 1985; Hewitt and Jancar, 1986).

Difficult or bizarre behaviour is even more difficult to classify, measure, and relate to patterns of behaviour in non- retarded populations.

EPIDEMIOLOGY OF SERVICES FOR MENTAL RETARDATION

Definitions for the study of services may be 'global' or 'partial'. In some communities there is a specified, comprehensive 'mental retardation service', but in most there is a mixture of specialist and generic agencies, facilities, personnel, and programmes. Study of the services is very important and has been much neglected. They are in hectic transition; client groups are not consistent with each other, nor do they stay the same; the characteristics of new services, like old ones, may be designed more on ideological, pragmatic, financial, or even whimsical criteria. Epidemiology can help to clarify the characteristics of their clients in terms of both impairments and disabilities; it can assess the degree to which a community based service encompasses all those with appropriate needs in the population served; it can relate the characteristics of services, including personnel, to client experience; it can monitor changes against objectives; it can evaluate the impact of service developments on the population of handicapped people, and upon other services.

This has been an important area of work in recent years, but the reproducibility of methods is still at issue, rather than the transferability of findings. Evaluation of facilities, programmes, interventions, and techniques is receiving ever greater emphasis, especially cost-benefit studies. Preventive programmes have been studied, including screening for metabolic disorder and hypo-thyroidism, dietary supplementation for neural tube defects, and immunisation, and so has pre-natal diagnosis and abortion. The most important total community service evaluation is that from Sheffield (Heron and Myers, 1983), but many studies of particular aspects of care have been reported from Wales (e.g. Humphries et al., 1986) and elsewhere. Sheffield, like Salford and Camberwell, have a long established Register upon which such studies can be based (Fryers, 1984; Wing and Hailey, 1972), but there are many more District Registers which were not set up for research, but which might facilitate evaluation if properly exploited (Fryers, 1983; Cubbon, 1986).

There is a great need for more concerted, long-term, scientifically rigorous, independent, comparative evaluation of care systems, management structures, and professional activities. We may be convinced of the rightness of the current philosophy directing planning of services, but attitudes, perceptions and philosophies will change, and unless we have established a body of reliable scientific information, there will be nothing to resist them.

CONCLUSIONS: POINTERS TO THE FUTURE

In conclusion it is worth suggesting what seem likely to be the most fruitful activities for epidemiologists in the field of mental retardation in the future. The establishment of reliable population frequencies for the many organic syndromes relating to retardation would benefit the pursuit of causes, and would provide the essential baseline data without which future preventive programmes can not be evaluated. It will need collaborative research covering a very large population, but the quality of data in many service laboratories is already very high. Peri-natal research should probably concentrate on the determinants of low birth weight.

More cohort studies would allow us to know more about the natural history of impairments, disabilities, and handicaps, and facilitate positive interventions. The studies of public perceptions, attitudes, professional practices, and social systems as they determine selection as 'retarded', might help us both to understand the social processes involved, and 'manage' them better in the interests of clients. Similarly, more careful study of specific disabilities and handicaps should stimulate action towards their amelioration. The disadvantages accruing for parents and families should have much more research emphasis, and service research should be given a much higher priority, if we are ever to claim scientific backing for what we provide for retarded people and their families.

All this will take resources; much more money is needed for proper epidemiological research in this field, but it might be wasted if we do not also attract high quality research staff, and provide a much better research training than we have done up to now, for those many professionals who do *some* research.

REFERENCES

Abel, E. L. and Sokol, R. J. (1986) Fetal alcohol syndrome is now leading cause of mental retardation. *Lancet,* **2,** 1222.

Berger, M. & Yule, W. (1985) IQ tests and assessment. In A. M. Clarke, A. D. B. Clarke and J. M. Berg (Eds.) *Mental Deficiency: The Changing Outlook,* 4th Edn. London: Methuen, pp. 53-98.

Blomquist, H. K., Gustavson, K. H. & Homgren, Nordenson, I., & Sweins, A. (1982) Fragile site X chromosomes and X linked mental retardation in severely retarded boys in a northern Swedish county: a prevalence study. *Clinical Genetics,* **24**, 393-8.

Blomquist, H. K., Gustavson, K. H. & Holmgren, Nordenson, I., and Palsson-Strae, U. (1983), Fragile X syndrome in mildly mentally retarded children in a northern Swedish county: a prevalence study. *Clinical Genetics,* **25,** 147-52.

Carr, J. (1985) The effect on the family of a severely mentally handicapped child. In A. M. Clarke, A. D. B. Clarke and J. M. Berg, (Eds.) *Mental Deficiency: The Changing Outlook,* 4th Edn. London: Methuen, pp. 512-48.

Carter, G .& Jancar J. (1983) Mortality in the mentally handicapped: a 50 year survey at the Stoke Park Group of Hospitals, 1930-80. *Journal of Mental Deficiency Research,* **27,** 143-56.

Cavazutti, G. B., Ferrari, P. & Lalla, M. (1984) Follow up study of 482 cases with convulsive disorders in the first year of life. *Medical Child Neurology,* **24,** 425-437

Clarke, A. M. (1985) Polygenic and environmental interactions. In A. M. Clarke, A. D. B. Clarke and J. M. Berg (Eds.) *Mental Deficiency: The Changing Outlook,* 4th Edn. London: Methuen, pp. 267-90.

Cooper, B. (Ed.) (1981) *Assessing the Handicaps and Needs of Mentally Retarded Children,* London: Academic Press.

Cooper, B., & Ort, M. (1983) Clinical and social characteristics of severely mentally retarded school age children in Mannheim. In M.M. Schmidt, and H. Remschmidt, (Eds.) *Epidemiological Approaches to Child Psychiatry, II.* Stuttgart: Thieme. pp.151-162.

Cooper, B., Jennen-Steinmetz, C., Lackus B., & Ort M. (1987) Patterns of impairment and disability in mentally retarded children: a study in Mannheim. In B. Cooper (Ed.) *Psychiatric Epidemiology,* London: Croom Helm, pp. 267-284.

Corbett, J. A. (1981) Prevention of mental retardation. In B. Cooper (Ed.) *Assessing the Handicaps and Needs of Mentally Retarded Children,* London: Academic Press, pp. 241-250

Corbett, J. (1985) Mental retardation; psychiatric aspects. In M. Rutter and L. Hersov (Eds.) *Child and Adult Psychiatry: Modern Approaches,* 2nd Ed. Oxford: Blackwell, pp. 545-566.

Cubbon, J. (1986) Planning community based services for mentally handicapped people. In N. Malin (Ed.) *Reassessing Community Care* London: Croom Helm, pp. 97-115.

Der, G .& Wooff, K. (1986) Effects of population mobility on register data. In G. H. M. M. den Horn, R. Giel, W. Gulbinat and J. H. Henderson (Eds.) *Psychiatric Case Registers 1960-1985,* Amsterdam: Elsevier, pp. 338-342.

Diaz-Fernandez, F. & Gestal-Otero, J. J. (1987) The influence of habitat on the prevalence of mental handicap. *International Journal of Epidemiology,* **16,**52-56.

Dupont, A. (1980) A study concerning the time related and other burdens when severely handicapped children are reared at home. *Acta Psych. Scand. Suppl.,* **285, 62**, 249-57.

Evans, J. A .& Hamerton, J. L. (1985) Chromosome anomalies. In A. M. Clarke, A. D. B. Clarke and J. M. Berg (Eds.) *Mental Deficiency: The Changing Outlook,* 4th Edn. London: Methuen, pp. 213-66.

Froster-Iskenius, U., Feisch, G., Schirren, C. & Schwinger, E. (1983) Screening for fra(X) (q) in a population of mentallyretarded males. *Human Genetics,* **63,** 153-7.

Fryers, T. (1983) *Standardisation of District Mental Handicap Registers,* Ass. Prof. Ment. Hand. People. London: King's Fund Centre.

Fryers, T. (1984) *The Epidemiology of Severe Intellectual Impairment: the Dynamics of Prevalence.* London: Academic Press.

Fryers, T. (1986a) Factors affecting prevalence of severe mental retardation. In J. Berg (Ed.) *Science and Service in Mental Retardation,* London: Methuen, pp. 3-14.

Fryers, T. (1986b) Survival in Down's syndrome. *Journal of Mental Deficiency Research,* **30,** pp. 101-110.

Fryers, T. (1987) Epidemiological issues in mental retardation.*Journal of Mental Deficiency Research,* **31,** 365-384.

Fryers, T. (1988) Pre- and Peri-natal Causes of Mental Retardation. In M. Kiely (Ed.) *Reproductive and Peri-natal Epidemiology.* New York: CRC Press.

Gillberg, C. Persson, E. Grufman, M. & Themner, U. (1986) Psychiatric disorders in mildly and severely mentally retarded urban children and adolescents. Epidemiological aspects. *British Journal of Psychiatry,* **149,** 68-74.

Gostason, R. & Akesson, H. O. (1986) Epidemiological and psychiatric aspects of mental retardation: a Swedish population study. In J. Berg (Ed.) *Science and Service in Mental Retardation,* London: Methuen, pp. 111-23.

Heron, A. & Myers, M. (1983) *Intellectual Impairment: The Battle Against Handicap.* London: Academic Press.

Hewitt, K. E.& Jancar, J. (1986) Psychological and clinical aspects of ageing in Downs Syndrome. In J. Berg (Ed.) *Science and Service in Mental Retardation.* London: Methuen, pp. 370-379.

Humphries, S., Lowe, K & de Paiva, S. (1986) *Long TermEvaluation of Services for Mentally Handicapped People in Cardiff:* Progress Report. Cardiff: Mental Handicap in Wales Applied Research Unit.

Illsley, R. and Mitchell, R. J. (1984) (Eds.) *Low Birth Weight.* London: Wiley.

Jacobs, P. A., Mayer, M., Matsuura, J., Rhoads, F. & Yee S. C. (1983) A cytogenetic study of mentally retarded males with special reference to the marker (X) syndrome. *Human Genetics,* **63,** 139-48.

James, F. E. & Snaith, R. P. (1979) *Psychiatric Illness and Mental Handicap.* London: Gaskell Press.

Jarvis, F. E. & Hey, E. (1984) Measuring disability and handicap due to cerebral palsy. In F. Stanley and E. Alberman (Eds.) *The Epidemiology of the Cerebral Palsies.* Oxford: Spastics International and Blackwell.

Kiely, M. (1984) Descriptive epidemiology of cerebral palsy. *Public Health Review,* **12, 1,** 79-101.

Kushlick, A. (1961) Subnormality in Salford. In M. W. Susser and A. Kushlick (Eds.) *A Report on the Mental Health Service of the city of Salford for 1960.* Salford: Health Dept.

Lancet, (1986) Preventive screening for fragile X syndrome. Editorial, *Lancet,* **2,** 1191-2.

Leck, I. (1983a) Spina bifida and anencephaly: fewer patients, more problems. *British Medical Journal,* **286,** 1679-80.

Leck, I. (1983b) Fetal malformations. In S.L. Barron, and A.M. Thomson (Eds.) *Obstetric Epidemiology.* London: Academic Press.

Livingstone, J. & Lyall, H. (1986) Contribution of fetal alcohol syndrome to mental retardation. *Lancet,* **2,** 1337-8.

Lubin, R. A. & Kiely, M. (1985) Epidemiology of aging in developmental disorders. In M. P. Janicki and H. R. Wisnievsky (Eds.) *Aging and Developmental Disorders, Baltimore:* Brookes, pp. 95-114.

Maclean, J. M. (1987) Early embryo loss. *Lancet,* **1,** 1033-4.

McCormick, M. C. (1985) The contribution of low birth weight to infant mortality and childhood morbidity. *New England Journal of Medicine,* **312,** 82-90.

Mercer, J. R. (1985) Social system perspective and clinical perspective: frames of reference for understanding career patterns of persons labelled as mentally retarded. *Social Problems,* **13,** 18-34.

Mercer, J. R. (1970) Sciological perspectives on mild mental retardation. In H. C. Haywood (Ed.) *Social-cultural aspects of mental retardation.* New York: Apppleton-Century-Crofts. Re-printed 1981 in W. Swann (Ed.) *The Practice of Special Education*

Mulcahy, M., O'Connor, S. & Reynolds, A. (1983) Census of the mentally handicapped in the Republic of Ireland (1981) *Irish Medical Journal,* **76, 2,** 71-75.

Neugebauer, R. & Susser, M. W. (1979) Epilepsy: some epidemiological aspects. *Psychological Medicine,* **9**, 207-215.

O'Connor, N. (1965) The prevalence of mental defect. In A. M. Clarke and A. D. B. Clarke (Eds.) *Mental Deficiency: The Changing Outlook.* 2nd Edn. London: Methuen.

Richardson, S. A. (1978) Careers of mentally retarded young persons: services, jobs, and inter-personal relations. *American Journal of Mental Deficiency,* **82,** 349-358.

Richardson, S. A. (1980) Growing up as a subnormal young person: a follow-up study. In S. A. Mednick and A. E. Baert (Eds.) *An Empirical Basis for Primary Prevention: Prospective Longitudinal Research in Europe.* London: OUP, pp. 262-267.

Richardson, S. A. (1987) The ecology of mental handicap. *Journal of the Royal Society of Medicine,* 80, 203-206.

Richardson, S. A. & Koller, H. (1985) Epidemiology. In A. M. Clarke, A. D. B.

Clarke and J. M. Berg (Eds.) *Mental Deficiency: The Changing Outlook,* 4th Edn. London: Methuen, pp. 356-400.

Roberts, R. (1986) *Imprisoned Tongues.* Manchester: Manchester University Press.

Roman, E. & Stevenson, A. C. (1983) Spontaneous abortion. In S. L. Barron and A. M. Thomson, Eds. *Obstetrical Epidemiology.* London: Academic Press, pp. 61-88.

Russell, O. & Hall, V. (1980) *Mental Handicap and Functional Disability* Research Report 6, Bristol: Dept. of Mental Health, University of Bristol.

Sorel, F. M. (1974) *Prevalence of Mental Retardation.* Netherlands: Tilburg University Press.

Stanley, F. & Alberman, E. (1984) *The Epidemiology of the Cerebral Palsies.* Oxford: Spastics International and Blackwell.

Stein, Z.& Susser, M. W. (1975) Public health and mental retardation: new power and new problems. In M. J. Begab and S. A. Richardson, (Eds.) *The Mentally Retarded and Society: A Social Science Perspective.* Baltimore: UPP, pp. 53-73.

Turner, G., Robinson, H., Laing, S. & Purvis-Smith, S. (1986) Preventive screening for the fragile X syndrome. *New England Journal of Medicine,* **315,** 607-9.

Webb, T. P., Bundey, S., Thake, A. and Todd, J. (1986) The frequency of the fragile X chromosome among school children in Coventry. *Journal of Medical Genetics,* **23,** 396-399.

Wilkin, D., (1979) *Caring for the Mentally Handicapped Child.* London: Croom Helm.

Wilkin, D. (1981) A task-oriented approach to the assessment of the distribution of the burden of care, levels of support and felt needs in the family. In B. Cooper (Ed.) *Assessing the Handicaps and Needs of Mentally Retarded Children,* London: Academic Press, pp. 185-96.

Wing, L. & Gould J. (1978) Systematic recording of behaviour and skills of retarded and psychotic children. *Journal of Autistic Developmental Disability,* **9,** 11-29.

Wing J. K. and Hailey, A. M. (1972) *Evaluating a Community Psychiatric Service: The Camberwell Register, 1966-71.* London: OUP.

WHO, (1980) *International Classification of Impairments, Disabilities, and Handicaps.* Geneva: World Health Organisation.

Wood, P. H. N. & Badley, E. M. (1978). An epidemiological appraisal of disablement. In A. E. Bennett,(Ed.) *Recent Advances in Community Medicine,* London: I. Churchill Livingstone, pp. 149-73.

CHAPTER 3

For Whom is Amelioration and Secondary Prevention Intended in Mild Mental Handicap? *

Stephen Richardson

Department of Pediatrics, Albert Einstein College of Medicine of Yeshiva University, Bronx, NY

INTRODUCTION

In thinking about secondary prevention and amelioration of those who are mildly mentally handicapped (hereafter referred to as MMH), there is rarely any consideration of who should be included under this rubric (but see in particular chapter 2). Perhaps this is because it has been assumed that at different times and places the same number and kinds of people will be identified as MMH. There is some backing in the conventional wisdom for the belief that the proportion or prevalence of MH is a uniform phenomenon. In 1962 President Kennedy's panel on mental retardation estimated that 3% of the population are MH and this prevalence rate is still widely quoted (The President's Panel, 1962). If this assumption is found to be incorrect then the scope and forms of prevention and amelioration will have to be considered in relation to the variation in the numbers and kinds of persons who are identified as MMH at different times and places.

One way of checking whether the prevalence of MMH is constant across time and place is to examine the prevalence rates found in epidemiological studies of defined geographical areas. We carried out this exercise and found the prevalence rates for MMH to range from 3.76 - 70/1000. All these studies were of children around the ages of 8 - 14 (Gruenberg, 1964; Kushlick and Blunden, 1974;

*This study was supported by the Foundation for Child Development, the William T. Grant Foundation, the National Institute of Child Health and Human Development, Grant No. HD07907, the G. Harold and Leila V. Mathers Charitable Foundation, the Charitable Trust of Mrs. Abby R. Mauze, the Scottish Home and Health Department, and the Social Science Research Council of the United Kingdom. The author wishes to thank R. Illsley, J. McLaren, and the late G. Horobin of the British Medical Research Council for their help and support.

Richardson and Koller, 1985). This finding of a seventeen fold difference is at first sight disconcerting and makes the question, "For whom is amelioration and secondary prevention intended in MMH?" worthy of serious consideration. Perhaps some clues may be obtained by trying to account for the extraordinary range of prevalence rates found for MMH children.

The period prior to the mid-1960s. The early studies were carried out before most communities had a service system to deal with mental handicap in children, especially those living at home and in the MMH range. A purpose of these early studies was to provide estimates for local authorities who wished to plan special educational facilities in the schools. The study of Gruenberg in Onondaga County, New York, is an example of a high prevalence study, of how MH was defined, and how cases were identified (New York State Department of Mental Hygiene, 1955).

"*Definition of a Case of Mental Retardation*. The specific sign and symptoms included under the rubric "retardation" are heterogeneous, confused and confusing because retardation is a word covering a variety of symptom manifestations which reflect many patterns of troublesome development. The reported children have in common the fact that they need special attention because they are having difficulty acquiring one or another of the skills of living which the responsible person regards as important (p. 86).

To identify cases, "responsible child care agencies were requested to report all children under 18 years of age, and residents of Onondaga County on March 1, 1953, identified as definitely mentally retarded, or suspected of mental retardation on the basis of developmental history, poor academic performance, IQ score, or social adaptation when contrasted with their age peers.

In practice, the interpretation of this definition of a "case" undoubtedly differed with the reporting agency. It is believed that reporting errors probably resulted in a greater inclusion of false positives than exclusion of false negatives (p. 87)".

In Onondaga County, the prevalence of MMH in children age 10-15 was approximately 70 per 1,000.

RECENT STUDIES

By the late 1960s and 1970s, a large number of communities had established MH services for mildly and severely MH children and procedures for the identification of children who they felt would benefit from special education. The two criteria used to define MH were IQ and adaptive behaviour. In practice, adaptive behaviour was how the child performed at school. Teachers were asked to identify children who were not meeting their standards of minimum school performance, and these children were then given a psychometric assessment and sometimes a medical examination. Based on these data, a clinical decision was made whether to classify the child as MH. In some communities, IQ testing was widely used in the school system. Of the two criteria employed in the definition of MH, there are indications that in the USA more weight was given to school performance. However, investigators of prevalence during this period often defined a child as mentally handicapped if the child had been classified by the local authorities and put in a special school or other placement for MH persons. This was, then an administrative definition of MH. Studies during this period produced prevalence rates for ages 10-14 that ranged from 15 to 35/1,000, with studies in the US more often having the higher prevalence. Most prevalence rates were between 20-30/1,000.

The convergence of prevalence rates led some to believe that there was a "true" prevalence of MH and that the differences between the studies could be accounted for by differences in methods used by the epidemiologist. The "true" prevalence belief appeared to stem from a conceptual model that MH is largely an innate characteristic of the individual rather than the resultant of some interaction between the individual and the environment, both social and biological.

There is some danger that once some prevalence rate, say 3%, is widely accepted, studies will find prevalence rates around 3%, in part because of factors that create self-fulfilling prophecies. Once the local authorities set up a system of MH services that are staffed, housed and financed, it is natural to want to use fully the facilities created and find enough children for this purpose. The development of psychometric testing can lead to the numbers identified being a function of the test used. If the test conforms to a normal curve, and MH is defined as more than two standard deviations below the mean, then approximately 25/1,000 will test as MMH if the population tested has the same characteristics as the population in which the test was standardized.

The studies in the 1980s have largely been conducted in Scandinavia. These have prevalence rates of 7-14/1,000, and some show lower prevalence rates for mild than for severe mental handicap. These rates were so much lower than those of other studies, that the Kennedy Foundation in the United States sent over a panel of inquiry. They were interested to see whether the very low prevalence rates for MMH might reflect a real drop due to the high standard of living and a comprehensive set of social services.

CHANGING SOCIAL CONDITIONS

During the early and middle periods of prevalence studies that were described, there was widespread practice and acceptance of the segregation of MMH children in schools and residences. MH was only one reason for segregation, e.g. physical disabilities, epilepsy, blindness and deafness. In the case of MH, the earlier beliefs promulgated by the eugenics movement provided a rationale for the segregation. Over the past two decades, the conventional wisdom of segregation has slowly given way to contrary beliefs that may be summarised by such terms as integration, mainstreaming and normalisation, both in services and in everyday living. The Scandinavian countries provided much of the impetus and examples for this shift. These changes in values have been accompanied by a lessening of prejudices and stereotypes held about MH children.

With the growing recognition that social environmental conditions influence the development of MMH children, there has been a shift in responsibility for MMH children from medical to educational and social work authorities.

There has been a growing awareness of the stigmatising consequences of classifying children as MH. The term "labelling" has been used and has a more pejorative connotation than "classifying". Several consequences stem from this awareness.

a) IQ testing, which was widely used, accepted, and at times revered, is now used less, and with more scepticism, and there is awareness that the test results may have stigmatising consequences.

b) It has been reported that in Scandinavia, psychologists sympathetic to the concepts of normalisation and mainstreaming have become more lenient in interpreting answers they receive when testing, and this practice may lead to higher scores being obtained.

c) Teachers are now more reluctant to bring to the attention of school authorities children they identify as having difficulty meeting minimal expectations for school performance.

d) There is recognition that the segregation of MH children may deprive them of important experiences that will assist their socialisation.

e) In earlier times parents had little or no say in the evaluation of educational placement of their children. They have now organised themselves into pressure groups and in some countries have statutory rights e.g. the UK and play a role in decision-making about what may be the best course for their child to follow.

f) There have been changes in the educational systems which include teaching styles and classroom sizes that make possible a greater heterogeneity of abilities of children in the same classroom.

g) Over the years the IQ cut-off point for MH has become lower, with 70 being the present level. Early studies used 75 and as high as 85 when the borderline range was included. Over the same period, an upward drift in test performance has been found. Both of these changes will, over time, show fewer children to be MH on psychometric grounds.

h) It is reasonable to expect that with all these changes there will now be children in regular classes not identified as MMH, who previously would have been classified as MMH and counted in prevalence studies.

The Scandinavians have been in the forefront of the changes that have been outlined. These changes have created problems for Scandinavians who have carried out prevalence studies of mental retardation. For example, in an epidemiological study, Hagberg et al. (1981) recognised, in the light of the social conditions that have been described, that they could not rely on administrative classification of MMH, because the cases found in administrative registers would not include a number of children who remained in regular classes under policies of mainstreaming and normalisation. They decided to define MMH as any child in the city of Gothenburg with an IQ between 50 and 70. The only way in which they could positively identify all these children would be by giving IQ tests to all children. This was not possible, both on grounds of lack of acceptability of widespread IQ testing and because of lack of funding. The second criterion of MH of adaptive behaviour was omitted from the definition. The investigators included all children in the mental handicap register in the defined IQ range and children who were known to hospitals. To try and find children in regular classes in the defined IQ range, they asked the school nurses and psychologists to identify children they thought were MH. IQs for these children were then obtained, and, if they were between 50 and 70, the children were included in the study. They found 72 children who had been classified as MH and were in MH facilities, and a further 19 from regular classes. This gave a prevalence rate of MMH of 3.7 per thousand. However, given these methods it would not have been possible for the investigators to ascertain with any certainty the number of children with IQ 50-70 who might have been missed. Further, without knowing the IQs of all children in the population, it was not possible to know how different the distribution of scores in Gothenburg was from the population on which the IQ test was standardised. There is evidence that there had been an upward drift in scores which would result in a smaller number of children with IQ 50- 70.

Zigler and Hodapp (1986) point to evidence that suggests the Swedish prevalence of MMH for children may be an underestimate.

In a study in Sweden by Granat and Granat, the IQ test scores of 19 year old males were examined during mandatory induction into the armed forces. Young men already in the Swedish MH register were excluded. Those tested had never been classified as MH, and approximately 15/1,000 scored below 70 in the IQ test given at age 19. If the figure is combined with those registered as MH, the overall prevalence rate is about 20/1,000. While these difficulties in determining prevalence rates were encountered in Scandinavia, with the general social changes described earlier, these difficulties will now also occur in other Western industrial societies.

Identifying MMH in Adults. There are a number of issues that need to be considered in defining and identifying MMH in adulthood. A psychometric definition of IQ between 50-70 which was used in the Scandinavian studies of children is impracticable because IQ testing of all adults would not be acceptable and might well be resented. A second possibility is to define all adults who were classified as MMH as children as continuing to MMH as adults. This also is impractical because it requires obtaining the childhood histories of all adults. This would probably be unacceptable as an invasion of an individual's privacy through identifying information most individuals would wish to be confidential and they would fear possible stigmatisation. For these and other reasons it has been customary to define MMH adults as those in MH services with IQs of 50 and above. These individuals come to the attention of local authorities in two ways. The first is when it is decided at school leaving age that a MMH young person will be unable to cope with finding or holding a job in the open job market. The second is when a MMH young person attempts to work in the open job market after leaving special school, encounters difficulties and failure, and comes to the attention of authorities who place adults in MH services. From age-specific prevalence studies prior to the recent Scandinavian studies, there is good evidence that approximately half of all children classified as MH disappear from any further MH services after leaving special classes at school. For MMH, this would mean more than half cease to be considered as MMH when they become adults. This may well be because the adaptive behaviour or social competence criterion differs in childhood and adulthood. In childhood it meant meeting minimal expectations for school performance. This uniform criterion was possible because of compulsory school attendance for all children. In adulthood, the minimal societal expectations include:

a) achieving economic independence through holding a job or being a housewife supported by a spouse. Some unemployment and job turnover is acceptable.

b) not violating laws or social mores in outstanding ways. Those who do not meet these expectations and had a childhood history of MH are those considered for adult MH services.

Adults are not expected to meet a criterion of a certain level of job skill, and wide variation is acceptable. Thus there is greater flexibility in the kinds of roles adults may play compared to children. This flexibility enables many children who had problems in school performance to find jobs where the skills required in school are less important and other skills may be used.

In prevalence studies of MMH, the variability in who is included in different studies is likely to come from those at the upper end of the IQ range. It is the result of the lack of any clear differentiation between those who are and are not MMH, due to a wide borderline area. We may also expect some variability around IQ 50 where it may be difficult to make a decision as to whether a person should be classified below 50, or 50 and slightly over. A difficulty in using IQ measures around the upper and lower ends of the MMH range is the questionable stability of IQ over time. In the follow-up study described in our second chapter in this book, we assembled for our study population of all MH children, the Terman-Merrill test scores available for each child during his or her school career. We then took three age periods: 5-8, 9-11 and 12-15 years and made our best judgement from all the IQ scores for an IQ for each period. We found across these time periods that almost half of the children had IQ changes of 10 points or more.

The problem of clearly defining MMH and then finding all cases in a population who meet the definition is not limited to epidemiological studies, but is part of the broader issue of representativeness.

Consideration and planning of programs of amelioration and secondary prevention of MMH need to be based on sound knowledge of the lives of the MMH and the prevalence in the community. A part of this knowledge must derive from valid research findings. A necessary question in evaluating research is to ask how representative are the findings for all MMH in the geographical area studied. Findings that are not representative can give biased and misleading results. For example:

1) Studies of the marriages of those who are MMH have generally been based on those known to some service agency because of problems related to the marriage. Without studying those who do not come to the attention of agencies, the results will be biased in overstating the problems of adults with MMH who are married.

2) Studies of MH in institutions are difficult to interpret and compare, because it is not known how similar or different are those who either were considered and rejected for admission, or those who were never considered for admission. The presence of behaviour disturbance may increase the likelihood of admission to an institution.

3) Studies which select MH cases through parent organisations leave unknown how these cases and their families may differ from

MH children whose families do not belong to, or have contact with parent organisations.

CONCLUSIONS

In considering the issues discussed in this chapter, we have reached a number of tentative conclusions.

1. The comparison of prevalence rates of MMH serves little value unless this is done with knowledge of the context in which the study is undertaken. This context should include the study definition of MMH, the procedures used in finding all cases in a defined population at risk who meet the study definition, and the social circumstances and conditions existing at the time and place of the study. It also follows that in considering amelioration and secondary prevention, the scope of active programmes needs to take into account the environment as well as the individual.

2. The presence of MH is not solely the result of a process inherent to the person manifesting the disorder, as was thought for many years. Rather it is the result of an interaction between the characteristics of the individual and his or her social and biological environment over time.

3. While the comparison of prevalence rates across studies has very limited value, it may be useful to see if relationships or phenomena in one study are also found in other studies. This can be useful even when there is some difference in the overall prevalence of MH in the studies compared. The following are some examples of findings that were common to different studies.

a) A number of reviewers have pointed out that in studies that showed different prevalence rates of MH, there was a common finding of a sharp drop off in administrative prevalence at school leaving age (Gruenberg, 1964).

b) Most studies of prevalence find a higher prevalence of MH for boys than girls. In a recent review it was shown that for mild mental retardation the highest ratio of boys to girls was found at the upper end of the IQ range for MMH reported in each study (Richardson et al., 1986).

c) There is a higher rate of behaviour disturbance among MH populations than for those who are not MH (Koller et al., 1983).

The replication of these findings across studies is added evidence that they are not idiosyncratic to a particular time and place. By further study to see what may account for the associations, clues may be found to facilitate amelioration and secondary prevention. We made such an attempt for examples b and c given above and these are described in Richardson et al. (1985); and Richardson et al. (1986).

4. In reviewing our own research and that of others we have been struck by the wide range of variation within MMH populations. They vary not only across an IQ range of 20 or more points, but also on the kinds and severity of other disabilities. Perhaps the most common of these disabilities are in speech, language and behaviour disturbance, but some also have sensory impairments, physical disabilities, epilepsy and cerebral palsy. These disabilities may cause greater barriers to effective daily living than the intellectual disability and may be more effective targets of amelioration. Thinking about mental handicap has dealt largely with pathology. For purposes of amelioration, the talents and assets of the individual should also be considered, and amelioration may usefully take the form of developing and strengthening the social skills of an individual either through individual training and/or through providing a set of social conditions that will enhance socialisation.

5. In reviewing epidemiological studies of MMH, there is often a surprising lack of clarity in describing the purpose of the study. The need for a clear purpose is particularly important today when increasingly smaller prevalence rates are being reported. If so few children are defined as MMH, does this mean that amelioration and secondary prevention services should shrink with prevalence reduction?

It is likely that some children who would have been classified as MMH are no longer classified for reasons already explored. With the changes consequent to adopting social policies based on such concepts as mainstreaming and normalisation, a useful purpose may now be to examine the histories and qualities of life of the borderline children who now are not classified as MMH. We need to reconsider who are the children who have difficulties, for whom amelioration would be valuable and what forms of amelioration should be used and tested for effectiveness. The characteristics and needs of children vary widely and methods of intervention must take this variation into account. Finally, the question should be raised as to whether the concept of MMH has outlived its usefulness and whether it should not be replaced by a conception that is not restricted to a single form of impairment. The concept of developmental disabilities is a move in this direction.

REFERENCES

Gruenberg, E. M. (1964) Epidemiology. In H. A. Stevens & R. Heber (Eds.), *Mental Retardation*. Chicago: University of Chicago Press.

Hagberg, B., Hagberg, G., Lewerth, A., & Lindberg, U. (1981) Mild Mental Retardation in Swedish School Children. 1. Prevalence. *Acta Pediatrician Scandinavia,* **70**:441-444.

Koller, H., Richardson, S. A., Katz, M. & McLaren, J. (1981) Behavior disturbance since childhood in a five-year birth cohort of all mentally retarded young adults in a city. *American Journal of Mental Deficiency,* **87**, 4:386-395.

Kushlick, A. & Blunden, R. (1974) The epidemiology of mental subnormality. In A. M. Clarke and A. D. B. Clarke (Eds.). *Mental Deficiency. The Changing Outlook.* London: Methuen.

New York State Department of Mental Hygiene (1955) Mental Health Research Unit, A special census of suspected referred mental retardation, Onondaga County, New York. *Technical Report of the Mental Health Research Unit.* New York: Syracuse University Press.

Richardson, S.A., Katz, M. & Koller, H. (1986) Sex differences in the numbers of children administratively classified as mildly mentally retarded: An epidemiological review. *American Journal of Mental Deficiency,* **91**, 250-256.

Richardson, S. A. & Koller, H. (1985) Epidemiology. In A. M. Clarke, A. D. B. Clarke and J. Berg (Eds.) *Mental Deficiency: The Changing Outlook, 4th Edition.* London: Methuen.

Richardson, S.A., Koller, H. & Katz, M. (1985) Relationship of upbringing to later behavior and disturbance of mildly mentally retarded young people. *American Journal of Mental Deficiency,* **90**, 1-8.

The President's Panel on Mental Retardation (1962). *National Action to Combat Mental Retardation.* Report to the President. U.S. Government Printing Office.

Zigler, E. & Hodapp, R. M. (1986) *Understanding Mental Retardation.* Cambridge: Cambridge University Press.

CHAPTER 4

Primary Prevention of Severe Retardation

Eva Alberman

Department of Clinical Epidemiology, London Hospital Medical College, UK

INTRODUCTION

The prevention of severe mental retardation is currently one of the major research growth areas, and both exciting and exceedingly complex. Current approaches can be categorised in several ways. One way is to classify the preventive actions by the basic cause of the defect. First are preventive actions in conditions known to be multifactorially determined, like neural tube defects; secondly, in conditions arising from chromosomal anomalies; and thirdly, in those known to be due to single gene defects, where the explosive effect of advances in molecular biology is beginning to make itself felt. In each of these, preventive actions can be classed as first, those which are possible before conception and are therefore genuinely primary prevention; secondly, those carried out in pregnancy to identify affected fetuses, primarily with a view to continuing only those pregnancies free from the defect under consideration; and thirdly, those carried out in the neonatal period in order to identify treatable defects. The last two cannot strictly be considered as primary prevention but will be included in this account for completeness.

MULTIFACTORIALLY CAUSED CONDITIONS

These conditions are those in which both genetic and environmental factors play a role, and the example most relevant to severe mental defect is neural tube defects. In a population-based study from Hertfordshire, carried out for children born between 1965 and 1967 (Laxova et al. 1977), survivors with neural tube defects accounted for 5% of all those ascertained at 5 and 7 years as severely mentally retarded. The incidence of these vary with a number of environmental factors, some of which may be acting as an indicator of disadvantage, but there is also clearly a genetic predisposition, recurrence risks rising sharply after each affected pregnancy.

The approaches to the prevention of these conditions, which have been unduly common in the British Isles, have included environmental interventions, and methods of offering selective termination of affected pregnancies. Potentially the most exciting approach is that of dietary supplementation for the primary prevention of this condition. The rationale behind this stems from a series of papers by Smithells et al. (1981, 1983) and Laurence et al. (1980, 1981) pointing to evidence of apparently remediable vitamin deficiencies in mothers who have borne affected children. These data fit in also with descriptions of cyclical trends in its birth prevalence, some of which could be related to the presumed nutritional state of the mother in her own childhood (Baird, 1977) and some to the timing of the pregnancy in relation to conditions of famine, or near famine (Stein and Susser, 1976). It could also explain some of the apparent continuing current secular fall in the prevalence seen in many countries (Seller, 1987).

The possibility of remedying the postulated causal vitamin deficiencies has been tested in two different ways. One has been to enrol mothers who have had a previously affected child, and are therefore at high risk, into a trial of periconceptional vitamin supplementation, to be taken for some weeks before conception and continued for some weeks after. The results of this uncontrolled trial are, on the face of it, very convincing, in that the risk of recurrence in subsequent pregnancies in treated mothers has fallen by twofold in South- east England and threefold in a high risk area of Northern Ireland (Seller and Nevin, 1984). However, there remain methodological problems in that the mothers enrolling in these trials are self-selected and, however the data are analysed, there remains a suspicion that the results may be due to selection bias.

To overcome this problem a randomised controlled trial is underway of a similar protective regime in women who have had a previously affected infant (Wald and Polani, 1984). The results of this trial are still awaited, and it is hoped will answer the question of the efficacy of this preventive action. The assumption has been made in both trials that the results can be extrapolated from the group at high risk of recurrence to women who have had no previous affected children.

However, the mainstay of the preventive programmes as currently practised in the UK depend on the identification of affected fetuses, usually with a view to terminating their pregnancies. Although as noted earlier, this can hardly be regarded as primary prevention it does offer to mothers at high risk some reassurance that the birth of an affected child can be avoided, and this particular programme also offers to mothers at low risk the possibility of detecting, albeit against expectation, the presence of a fetus with a neural tube defect.

This screening of pregnancies is done in two stages. The first is a simple biochemical test to determine the level of alpha fetoprotein (AFP) assessed on the serum of the mother between the 16th and 20th weeks of pregnancy. This measurement discriminates well between the raised levels found in the presence of an abnormal opening in the spinal cord or brain, through which the fetal protein leaks, and the lower levels in a pregnancy without these or certain other defects.

In mothers found to have raised levels it is possible to confirm the presence of an affected fetus by means of a diagnostic quality ultrasound, or by extracting and testing a sample of the amniotic fluid which surrounds the fetus for raised levels of AFP. It has been shown that this programme can detect up to 85% of fetuses with an open defect, and that the more severe the lesion the more likely it is to be detected (Ferguson-Smith, 1987). It is of course up to the parents to choose whether they wish to terminate an affected pregnancy, but experience shows that most will wish to do so.

The acceptance of the tests will in part depend on the understanding of the parents of the screening system, and early enough attendance in pregnancy to profit from them. There is a danger with these and other complex screening devices that those families who by their social and educational circumstances stand to gain the most from them may be the last to be offered the choice that they made possible.

CHROMOSOMAL ANOMOLIES

About one third of cases of severe mental defects are secondary to the presence of Trisomy 21, Down's syndrome; a lesser but important proportion in boys due to the presence of a Fragile X chromosome; and a very small proportion due to the presence of other chromosomal anomalies.

Although the cause of none of these anomalies is known, we have enough knowledge to identify high risk groups, at least in the case of Down's syndrome and some cases of Fragile X. The most striking feature of the epidemiology of Down's syndrome is the marked rise of birth prevalence as maternal age rises, particularly after the age of 34. This knowledge gives us our best and simplest method of primary prevention, namely the encouragement to mothers to restrict child bearing to younger ages where the risk is low. Simply avoiding childbirth after the age of 34 would reduce the current level of Down's syndrome by some 30%.

If a mother chooses to, or accidentally becomes pregnant at a relatively advanced age, it is also possible to test for the presence of fetal trisomy, or many other anomalies, by withdrawing a sample of amniotic fluid after the 14th week of pregnancy, and culturing and then karyotyping the fetal cells found in that fluid. This test, albeit invasive and expensive, is simple enough and safe enough to offer to all mothers whose risk is markedly raised on the grounds of their age, usually after the age of 34, and this programme of offering diagnostic tests to older mothers is now available in most parts of the United Kingdom. More recently it has been found possible to sample chorionic villi at an earlier stage of pregnancy. Again these diagnostic tests can only lead to a decision about the avoidance, or termination of the affected pregnancy, but this is sometimes incorrectly regarded as primary prevention.

Although the risk in younger mothers is less than a tenth of that in older women, the very large number of births at younger ages means that the majority of affected births cannot be prevented by any means relating to an advanced maternal age. Recently it has been shown however that in pregnancies carrying Down's syndrome fetuses, the level of AFP in maternal serum is often unduly low between the 16th and 18th week of pregnancy, quite independently of the risk associated with maternal ageing. By combining an estimate of these two risks for an individual pregnancy, it becomes possible to identify in young women a high risk group, and in older women a low risk group, thus refining the prediction of high risk group for amniocentesis. It has been estimated that using a prediction based on a combination of levels of AFP and of maternal age will allow the identification of up to 40% of all cases (Cuckle et al., 1984), and that the addition of another test on maternal serum may increase this predictability to 60% (Wald, Cuckle et. al., 1988).

Again this could offer no more than the opportunity to offer the diagnostic testing of the fetal cells to a high risk group, and the possibility of selective termination, an offer which some may not feel is justified in conditions such as Down's syndrome.

We are also approaching a stage where the development of tests for the presence of the Fragile X syndrome will allow the reliable identification of its carriers and the subsequent informed decision about childbearing, as well as the presence of an affected X in a male fetus (Lancet, 1986).

SINGLE GENE DEFECTS

In an increasing number of the numerous single gene defects leading to severe mental defect, advances in molecular biology are also offering the possibility of identifying carriers of the deleterious genes, as well as affected fetuses. These conditions include those which are inherited in a recessive Mendelian fashion, where the disease will be passed on only by couples who are both carriers, and those which are inherited in a Mendelian dominant manner, and can therefore be found in children of couples of whom only one carries the gene. The latter is also true in the inheritance of sex-linked diseases, where the deleterious gene (or section of chromosome) is on the X chromosome.

The presence of carriers is best detected before conception, or even before marriage, but these can only be feasibly screened for in known high risk groups. In practice, in the present context this is largely restricted to such conditions at Tay Sachs disease, in which the prevalence of carriers in Ashkenazi Jews is common enough to warrant population screening, and the screening before child bearing of members of families known to be carrying a specific disease, such as Huntington's Chorea. In families where carriers have been identified the only method of primary prevention is abstention from pregnancy. Such programmes raise many and very significant social and ethical problems which need to be faced by affected families, and by society in general.

However, the previous birth of a child affected with such a disease or one of the mucopolysaccharide diseases may now be followed by prenatal diagnosis in a subsequent pregnancy, made possible by means of testing fetal cells removed by chorionic villus biopsy or by amniocentesis. Unfortunately such a programme will have less impact than one of identifying carriers before pregnancy, but this will not always be possible.

NEONATAL DIAGNOSIS

It should not be forgotten that some of the most effective forms of primary prevention of severe mental defect are those of avoidable conditions arising after birth. The prevention of accidents; of non-accidental injury; of infections of the brain or its covering membranes; and the excellent treatment of brain tumours will all contribute to a further reduction of this defect. Moreover many of these postnatal events are related to social circumstances and become less common when these improve.

CONCLUSIONS

In summary, in recent years there have been remarkable advances in the primary prevention, and the avoidance of the birth of individuals destined to become severely mentally retarded, and progress in the field is continuing unabated. Up to the present these measures have not had a substantial effect on the prevalence of such births, but over the next few years this is likely to become more perceptible. Such measures however require continuing research and service support, and the ongoing education of the public and professionals regarding the new developments.

REFERENCES

Baird, D. (1977) Epidemiologic patterns over time. In D.M. Reed & F.J. Stanley (Eds.) *The Epidemiology of Prematurity*. Baltimore-Munich: Urban and Schwarzenberg.

Cuckle, H. S., Wald, N. J. & Lindenbaum, R. H. (1984) Maternal serum alpha fetoprotein measurement: a screening test for down syndrome. *Lancet,* **1,** 926-929.

Ferguson-Smith M. A. (1987) Neural tube defects and Down's syndrome: a success and a failure. In: *Screening for fetal and genetic abnormality*. Kings's Fund Forum.

Lancet. (1986 (2)) Preventive Screening for Fragile X Syndrome. 1191-1192.

Laurence, K. M., James, N., Miller, M. & Campbell H. (1980) Increased risk of recurrence of pregnancies complicated by fetal neural tube defects in mothers receiving poor diets, and possible benefit of dietary counselling. *British Medical Journal,* **281,** 1592-1594.

Laurence, K. M., James, N., Miller, M. H., Tennant, G. B. & Campbell, H. (1981) Double-blind randomised controlled trial of folate treatment before conception to prevent recurrence of neural tube defects. *British Medical Journal,* **282,** 1509-1511.

Laxova, R., Ridler, M. A. C. & Bowen-Bravery M. (1977) An etiological survey of the severely retarded Hertfordshire children who were born between January 1 1965 and December 31 1967. *American Journal of Medical Genetics,* **1,** 75-86.

Seller, M. J. (1987) Nutritionally induced congenital defects. *Proceedings of the Nutrition Society,* **46,** 227-235.

Seller, M. J. & Nevin, N. C. (1984) Periconceptional vitamin supplementation and the prevention of neural tube defects in south-east England and Northern Ireland. *Journal of Medical Genetics,* **21,** 325-330.

Smithells, R. W., Nevin, N. C., Seller M. J., Sheppard, S., Harris, R., Read, A. P., Fielding D. W., Walker, S., Schorah, C. J. & Wild J. (1983) Further experience of vitamin supplementation for prevention of neural tube defects recurrences. *Lancet,* **1,** 1027-1031.

Stein, A. & Susser, M. (1976) Maternal starvation and birth defects. In S.Kelly, E. Hook, D. Janerich, and I.H. Porter (Eds.) *Birth Defects: Risks and Consequences.* New York: Academic Press.

Wald, N.J., Cuckle, H.S., Densem, J.W. et al. (1988) Maternal serum screening for Down's Syndrome in early pregnancy. *British Medical Journal,* **297,** 883-887.
Wald, N. J. & Polani P. E. (1984) Neural tube defects and vitamins: the need for a randomised clinical trial. *British Journal of Obstetrics and Gynaecology,* **91,** 516.

CHAPTER 5

The New Morbidity: Implications for Prevention and Amelioration

Alfred A. Baumeister and Frank Kupstas

John F. Kennedy Center for Research on Education and Human Development, Vanderbilt University, Tenn, USA

INTRODUCTION

Our charge is to address the role of social and environmental factors relative to prevention and treatment of mental handicap. While the focus here is on mild forms of mental handicap or retardation, degree of severity and type of handicap are difficult to isolate completely, especially regarding primary prevention. The basic proposition is that comprehensive theories of causation and effect need to be articulated and that, relative to prevention, arbitrary distinctions involving severity and type of disability should not be attempted. This is not to say that there is no such disorder as mental retardation, but from the perspective of primary prevention, particularly, we may have difficulty predicting one particular outcome as opposed to another. The model adopted here is that mental retardation is but one among a number of conditions that describe the 'new morbidities'.Within this conceptual framework, mental retardation is a 'symptom', among others, of underlying biological and social causes.

Prevention of mental retardation remains a highly publicized concept in Western societies. Indeed, in the United States, the President's Committee on Mental Retardation established a national goal to reduce by half the incidence of mental retardation by the year 2000. Another less well known objective is to reduce incidence and prevalence of mental retardation associated with 'social disadvantage' to the lowest possible level by the end of the century.

Several commentators have questioned whether these goals realistically can be accomplished (Clarke and Clarke, 1977; Zigler, 1978; Baumeister, 1981). The reasons include: (a) lack of scientific and technical knowledge, (b) vague understanding of incidence and prevalence, and (c) failure to implement effective public policies.

Furthermore, public policy that would propel us toward the goal of primary prevention must be couched in the context of political and economic realities.

A study of the history of mental retardation in the U.S. and Great Britain reveals that progress, scientific and social, has pursued a wavelike, even an erratic, course rather than a continuous linear trend. Research does, of course, influence development of service programs, but public policies, including systems of classification, are driven by prevailing social, political and economic climates and values (Baumeister, 1981). Have we made progress? On some fronts, yes; but in significant areas we, at least in the U.S., have lost ground.

DEFINITIONAL ISSUES

Definitions of mental retardation and accompanying systems of classification are based primarily on two related criteria: 'subaverage' intelligence and 'deficits' in adaptive behaviour (e.g., Grossman 1983). The American definition of mental retardation bears close similarities to the current British description of mental handicap. While this generally accepted approach to identification, diagnosis, and intervention is useful with respect to distribution of service resources, a bivariate definition in practice is deceptively simple and misleading because it fails to embrace and reveal the enormous variability with respect to cause, effect, degree and significance embedded in the concept of 'mental retardation'.

Mental retardation, among all the afflictions of human kind, may well be the most intricately complex constellation of circumstances with respect of causation, intervention and prevention. Many biological, behavioural and cultural variables interact to produce impairments in intellectual and social adaptation or, more generally, in quality of life. Sometimes these impairments are absolute in the sense that an individual will be considered handicapped in practically every environmental or social context - in short, a person who could not survive without special help.These represent the most severely involved cases that often, but not always, can be traced to biomedical causes.

In any event, most retarded people are identified in terms relative to generally accepted standards of behaviour for different age and cultural norms, in different contexts, and times. These, typically, are individuals whose retardation is apt to be considered mild or moderate and whose handicaps are most directly evident in school. Different environments define competence differently, a fact that must increasingly be reflected in systems of definition, classification, prevention, treatment, and research, as well as in policy decisions.

That there are a great many sources of mental retardation is well known to professionals, policy makers, and other concerned citizens. Several hundred biomedical etiologies have already been identified and described in the literature. Additional biological and environmental causes continue to be reported with great regularity. The Fragile X Syndrome, for instance, probably accounts for many who would have been diagnosed a few years ago as 'unknown prenatal influence'. However, the opportunity to isolate singular biological factors as causative agents and, therefore, to initiate cost-effective prevention and intervention programs is an illusion. The social and biological complexities must be addressed in a multivariate and coordinated program of research and prevention. Witness, for example, the tragedy that has overtaken us with respect to maternal PKU. Congenital defects associated with acquired immunodeficiency syndrome, strongly linked to SES and cultural factors, may soon displace Down's syndrome as the most common biomedical cause of mental retardation.

All disabilities must be considered in context. The putative causative agents are so diverse in origin, effect, timing and severity that each condition generally requires its own prevention and treatment measures. Moreover, diversity of biological cause and effect is such that disease models of mental retardation are not often interchangeable at a conceptual level, much less at a clinical one. Policies that drive research, service and prevention must take these complexities into account.

Even given that many cases of mental retardation are attributable to biological perturbations, the exact nature of these processes is unlikely to be clear in most cases. Thus, a general diagnosis such as 'slow fetal growth' may be used without any great revelation as to causative mechanisms. Even in cases clearly involving significant brain damage, most often aetiology cannot be specified and when causes are suggested, subsequent information shows that the original diagnosis is frequently in error (Baumeister and MacLean, 1979).

Evidence is becoming increasingly abundant that multivariate explanatory models, involving biological, social, and ecological variables linked together in a common matrix will ultimately provide a much more valid and useful basis to generate workable theories of cause and effect, on the one hand, and intervention and prevention strategies, on the other. Uncertainties about aetiology, symptomatology, and treatment will not yield to insular and simplistic unidimensional models. Even instances where a particular biological cause can be implicated, the ultimate outcome typically is multiply determined. Recent data show that babies at risk are differentially susceptible to problems of adaptation depending on social variables.

THE NEW MORBIDITY

Mental retardation and related developmental disabilities are characterized by a myriad of features and causal agents. It is this heterogeneity that makes amelioration and prevention challenging and frustrating. Genetic, behavioral, medical, social, and personal variables are all implicated in determining developmental outcomes and morbidity. We also know, but do not yet fully appreciate, how subtle interactions of different aetiologic factors impact on the fetus and, subsequently, on the growing child.

According to the National Institute of Child Health and Human Development (NICHHD), in the United States approximately 50% of moderate to severe mental retardation has a genetically determined component (National Institute of Child Health and Human Development, 1986a). Severe retardation results from inadequate development of the nervous system, brought about by genetic and/or environmental factors that interact and influence growth, differentiation, and maturation of neurons and synaptic functioning. These conditions include chromosomal abnormalities, inborn errors of metabolism, central nervous system irregularities, multiple congenital malformation syndromes caused by single genes, and syndromes of unknown etiology that follow established patterns of inheritance and those that are environmentally influenced.

At the same time we question a widely held assumption, at least in the U.S., that severe mental retardation cuts much more evenly across racial, ethnic, and geographic populations. The huge genetic component notwithstanding, data do not compel this conclusion and, in fact, certain groups are differentially at risk for severe retardation. Recently, Berg (1986) reviewed conditions of mental retardation arising from physical determinants of environmental origin. Various prenatal, perinatal and postnatal events were found to produce a variety of disabilities, and these, in turn, are linked to social and economic factors. For instance, there is an exceedingly high incidence of Fetal Alcohol Syndrome among Alaskan natives. The rate is about 50 per 1,000 births, as opposed to a national average of about 1.5 per 1,000 (Baumeister and Hamlett, 1985).

The first figure illustrates the connection between severe mental handicap and SES and race. We have deliberately excluded from these data those cases having a distinct biomedical aetiology. When one includes causes of severe disability, linked to socio-cultural variables, such as exposure to intoxicants, poor medical care, nutritional inadequacy, and accidents, class differences are even more marked.

Independent causal factors for mild mental retardation are more difficult to isolate owing to the fact that they are often of familial origin,and represent a social/cultural base in which subtle and complex interactions occur. This multi-factorial basis of mild retar

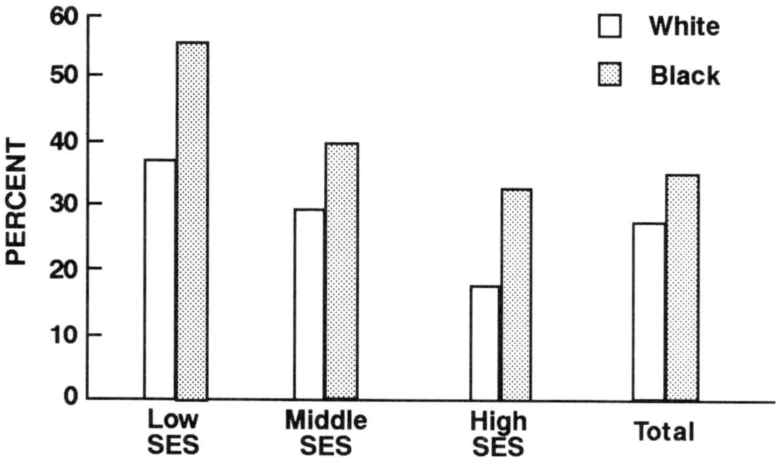

Figure 1
Percent of severely retarded children without major CNS disorders by socio-economic status. (Statistical data taken from: Collaborative Perinatal Project of the National Institute of Neurological & Communication Disorders & Stroke)

dation evades simple analysis because of the interplay between biological factors and environmental events that place a child at risk. Environmental contingencies tend to exacerbate biological risks, creating a synergism in which the combination of variables is much more influential than when viewed separately.

In 1975 Haggerty and colleagues introduced the concept: "New Morbidity"*. Conditions associated with the New Morbidity at that time were described as behavioural and school problems among children and adolescents. Also included were environmental risks, personal behaviour such as drug and alcohol abuse, and accidents. We have expanded the concept to encompass a wider array of psychosocial problems including violence, suicide, adolescent pregnancy, psychiatric symptoms, and chronic health disorders, along with school problems such as learning disabilities. While none of these problems is really new, what is most alarming about the New

*Their work was originally supported through the Division of Material and Child Health of the United States Health Resources and Services Administration.

Morbidity is the increasing prevalence of these conditions (Butler et al, 1984).

Traditional roles of pediatricians included prevention, diagnosis and treatment of acute and chronic illnesses, especially those arising from infectious diseases, however such illnesses have yielded to advances in public health services and new medical technologies

Today, the major thrust of preventive services is on behavioural problems and accidents. Behaviour disorders are now more prevalent than any single disease among children and adolescents. Conditions associated with the New Morbidity are becoming more pervasive and appear to be affecting children at younger ages. Figure 2 illustrates the percentage of children in the United States exhibiting some type of health disorder in 1986 (Children's Defense
Fund, 1986a). Between 5-10 million children under 21 years of age suffer from one or more health impairments including 1% hearing impaired, 1% visually impaired, 18% speech impaired, 30% other

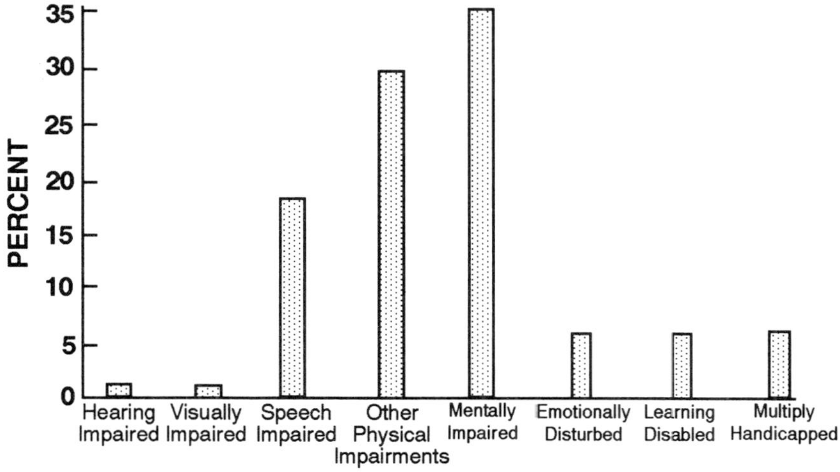

Figure 2
Percent of children in United States under 21 years of age suffering from selected health impairments. (Statistical data taken from: Building Health Programs for Teenagers, Children's Defense Fund, 1986)

physical health impairments including crippling conditions and chronic illness, 35% mentally impaired, 5% emotionally disturbed, 5% learning disabled and 5% multiply handicapped.

Aside from these health problems, childhood mental health disorders are on the increase in the U.S. as shown in Figure 3. According to U.S. government estimates, a 108% increase in childhood mental disorders was observed between 1980 and 1984 (National Center for Health Statistics, 1986a)

Unresolved problems in this area can also lead to chronic health disorders and violent behaviour as evidenced by the increasing amount of adolescent homicides and suicides. These data are

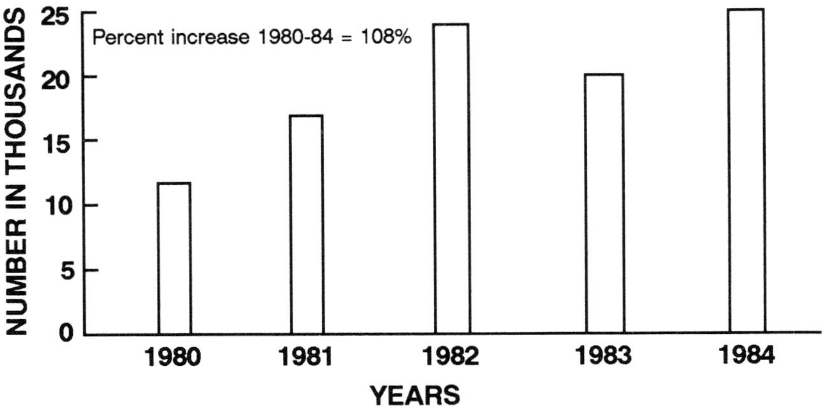

Figure 3
Number of diagnosed childhood mental disorders for the United States, 1980-84.
Source: Vital and Health Statistics (Series 13, No. 87),
National Center for Health Statistics.

shown in Figure 4. Between 1970 and 1983 in the United States, there was a 6% increase in homicides among children and adolescents between the ages of 5 and 24 years, and for the same age group and time period, suicides increased by 34% (National Center for

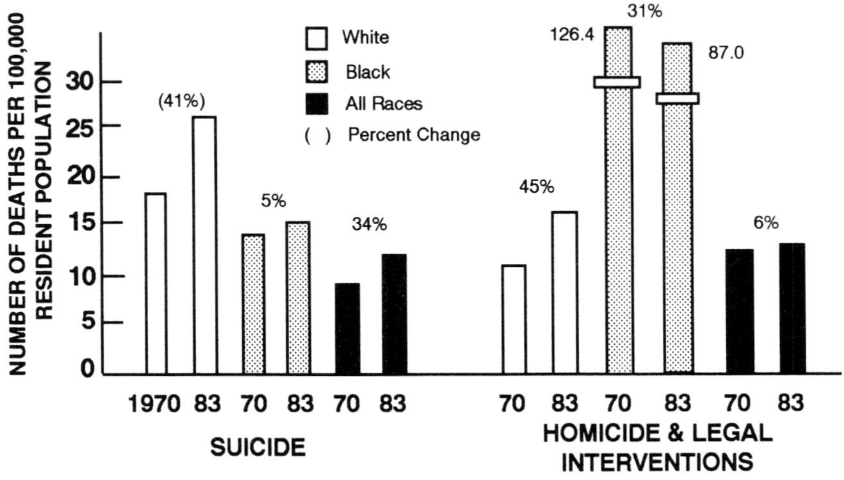

Figure 4
Death rates from suicide, homicide, and legal intervention, by race, ages 5-24, 1970 and 1983. (Statistical data taken from Vital Statistics of the United States, Vol. II, 1950-83, National Center for Health Statistics).

Health Statistics, 1984). Suicide rates among adolescents have increased every 5 years since 1950. Suicide is now the second leading cause of death in this population, taking more than 6,000 lives each year (Barth, 1986).

Statistics on drug use among youths aged 12 through 17 years for 1974 and 1982, indicate that for those who ever used cigarettes, there was a 5% decrease, which is good. However, the largest increase is among young people which includes girls of child-bearing age. For those who ever used alcohol there was a 21% increase, a 16% increase for marijuana, and those youths who ever used cocaine increased by 81%, which is not good (U.S. Bureau of the Census, 1985). These trends are shown in Figure 5.

Another interesting set of figures concerns the percentage of students in programs for the handicapped from 1977 through

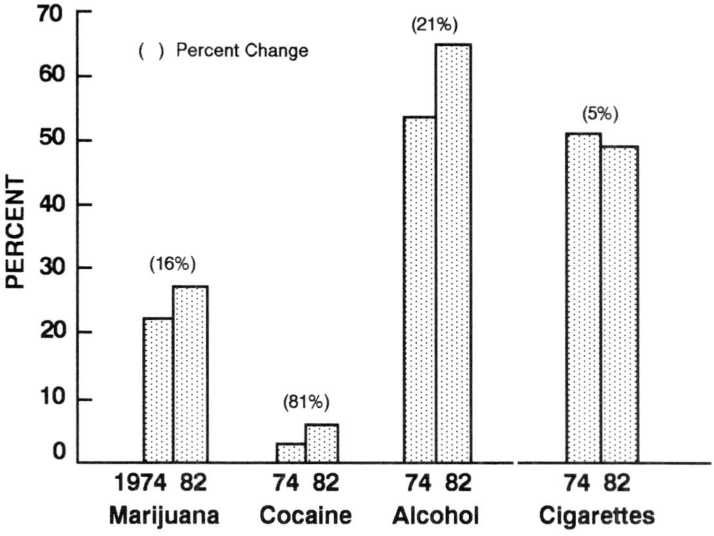

Figure 5
Percentage of youths who ever used drugs by type of drug, 1974 and 1982. (Source: Statistical Abstracts of the United States 1986 Bureau of the Census, Washington, DC.)

1984. During that period of time, the percentage enrolled in classes for the mentally retarded decreased by 35%, which may be good, but, for those in classes for the emotionally disturbed there was an 11% increase, and for learning disabled there was a 95% increase (U.S. Bureau of the Census, 1985). These data are shown in Figure 6. These changes must represent the effect of social pressures, not scientific progress. There is evidence suggesting a similar trend in Britain.

While the overall birth rate among teenagers in the United States declined by almost one-fourth from 1970 through 1983, birth rate

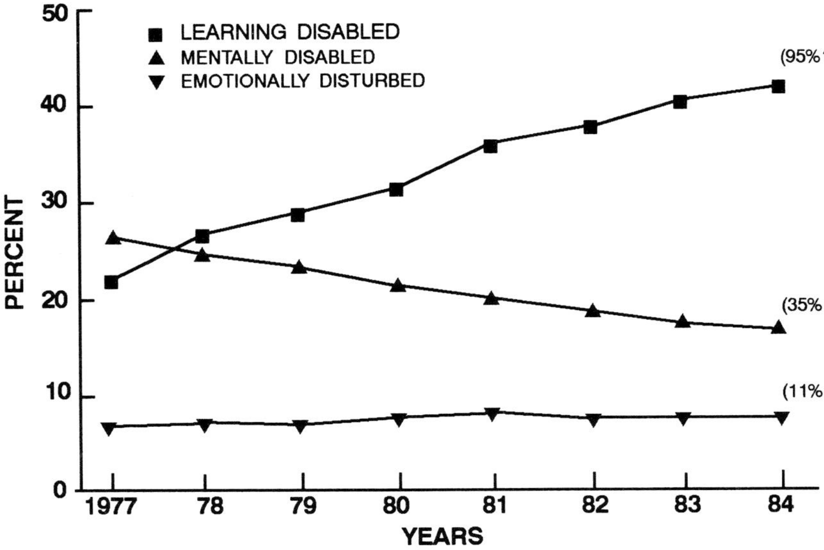

Figure 6
Percentage of elementary and secondary students in education programs for the handicapped, by type of handicap and percentage of change, 1977-84, (3-21 years old). (Source: Statistical Abstract of the United States 1986, Bureau of the Census, Washington, DC.)

for unmarried teenagers increased by more than one-third during the same time period. In 1970, 31% of teen births were to single mothers. By 1983 this figure was up to 53% and is still on the increase (Children's Defense Fund, 1986b).

The New Morbidity affects children from all socioeconomic levels; however, we estimate that children who live in poverty are between one and one-half to two times more likely than non-poor children to suffer from one or more disabilities (Children's Defense Fund, 1986a). In some instances, such as mental retardation, learning disabilities, and accidents the rates are much higher. This conclusion is supported by data shown in the next figure indicating that for individuals under 18 years of age who are experiencing limitations in major activities (that is, the capacity to work, keep house, and engage in preschool or school activities), more than twice as many are from families earning under $10,000 per year when compared with those families earning $35,000 or more per year. The same holds true for 5- through 17-year-old youths who are rated in fair or poor health, with a seven-fold increase for those individuals in the lower income group when compared with the higher income group (National Center for Health Statistics, 1986b).

At this point it would be helpful to index and describe some of the more conspicuous and powerful variables that affect the health and well being of a pregnant woman, possibly causing the delivery of

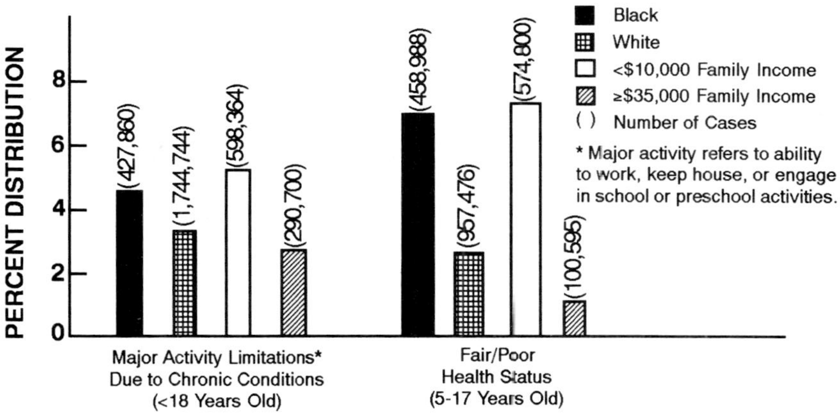

Figure 7
Major activity limitations and fair/poor health status according to selected characteristics, United States, 1983. (Statistical data from Vital and Health Statistics, Series 10, No. 154, 1983, National Center for Health Statistics).

of a high-risk infant. This will help explain what we mean by the New Morbidity, demonstrating certain aspects of our model, as shown in the next figure. Note here that this particular model, for convenience of explanation, is based on poverty and prematurity. This represents but one aspect of and but one use of viewing a very complex paradigm encompassing multiple variables.

We begin with what we will call Predisposing Variables. These are broken down into three sub-categories: demographic, behavioural,

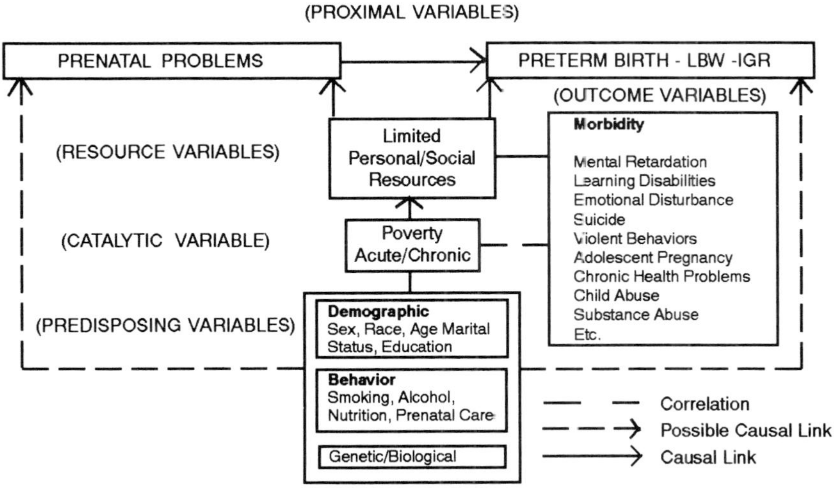

Figure 8
Selected variables having a relationship with poor pregnancy outcome, and subsequent morbidity.

and genetic/biological. Demographic factors include age,race, socioeconomic status, marital status, environment, and education. While these demographic variables are discussed separately, it is important to remember that they act in concert.

Age and marital status. There is overwhelming evidence that women under the age of 17 and over 34 years have an increased probability of delivering a high-risk infant (Institute of Medicine, 1985). While adolescence has not been shown to be a direct causative factor in preterm or LBW infants, these young mothers are more likely to be poor, in a minority group less well educated, unmarried, and receive late or inadequate prenatal care. While teenagers accounted for 13% of all U.S. births in 1985, they were responsible for approximately 18% of all the LBW infants born that year (National Center for Health Statistics, 1987).

The age factor in high-risk pregnancy is very complex. Recent studies in Europe report that prematurity and not LBW may be the more important variable associated with adolescent pregnancy. Controlling for gestational age, most LBW infants are found to be premature. The British Birth Study revealed a relationship between maternal age and prematurity but not low birthweight, and French data also indicate that prematurity is strongly related to low SES and maternal age. The same conclusions concerning prematurity and low SES were reached by a Council of Europe study for member states. Finally, Canadian studies showed both prematurity and low birthweight were associated with maternal age (Fedrick and Anderson, 1976; Fedrick and Adelstein, 1978; Makinson, 1985).

Race. Probably one of the most complex and perplexing factors concerning the delivery of a high-risk infant, especially LBW and preterm birth, is that of race. Even when other factors are taken into account such as education and age, when compared to white infants, blacks have a higher rate of LBW babies (Binkin et al., 1985; Geronimus, 1986; National Center for Health Statistics, 1985; Shiono and Klebanoff, 1986; Shiono et al., 1986). Figure 9 shows the number of LBW infants in the U.S. by race and by geographic region.

In a large-scale prospective study of 29,415 pregnancy outcomes, carried out by the Kaiser-Permanente health clinic (Shiono et al., 1986), whites, Hispanics, blacks, and Asians were compared for LBW. The results were 3.6% for whites, 4.0% for Hispanics, 5.6% for Asians, and 7.7% for blacks. While national averages for black and white LBW infants are higher, 12.5% and 5.6% respectively, one may conclude that the rate for blacks is about twice that for whites. In 1983, 1 out of every 8 black infants in the United States was low birthweight compared with 1 out of every 18 whites. For prematurity, the rates were 1 out of 6 for blacks, and 1 out of every 12 for

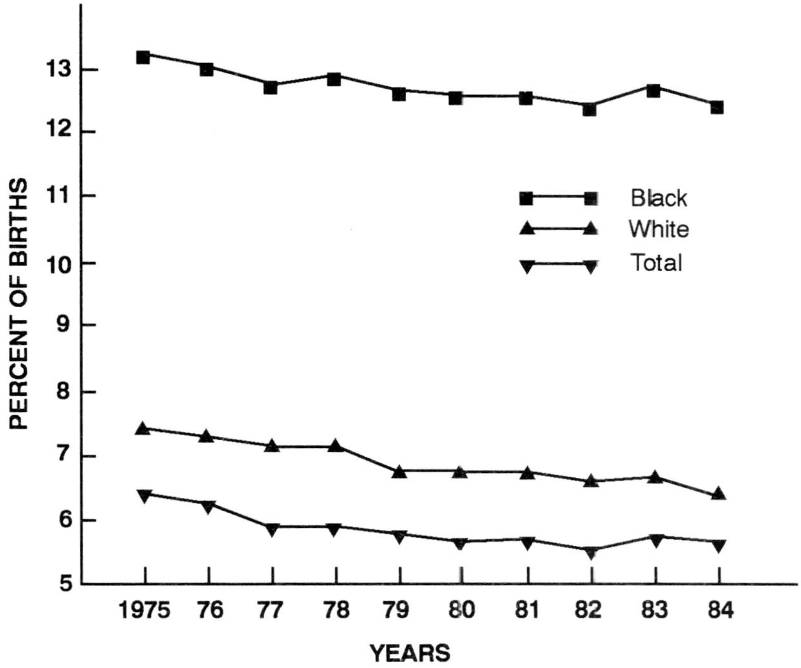

Figure 9
Percentage of low birth weight infants from total live births in U.S. 1975 through 1984.
(Source of statistical data: Statistical Abstract of the United States, 1987,
Bureau of the Census, Washington, DC.

whites (Children's Defense Fund, 1986c). While we know that many considerations contribute to higher rates for blacks, such as environmental, social, and personal risks, even when these factors are taken into account, the low birthweight rate for blacks is still significantly higher. Some researchers have concluded that biological and genetic factors alone may be responsible for a large number of these low birthweight infants. We do not believe that the available evidence compels this conclusion. In fact, there are data to the contrary.

Socioeconomic status. Whether measured by income, education, social class or census tract, socioeconomic status (SES) has been strongly linked to increased risk of preterm delivery and low birthweight (Institute of Medicine, 1985). Recent studies point to the connection between birth variables and subsequent development as modulated by social factors. We shall specifically mention one set of studies that controlled for genetic confounds. Wilson (1983; 1985) has recently presented data concerning risk and resilience in early development among samples of MZ and DZ twins. The low birthweight twins exhibited substantially lower IQs. But there was an interaction in which the upper SES twins recovered completely by the sixth year. The conclusion is that parental education and SES are powerfully related to 6-year IQ scores among at-risk infants.

The Institute of Medicine has compiled data between 1971-1981 on educational attainment of mothers, and race and the relative risk of LBW. The relative risk for delivering a LBW infant decreases sharply among mothers who have at least 12 years of education, for both whites and blacks. There is also evidence showing that poor children are much more likely to suffer from chronic conditions, attend school less often than non-poor children, their average length of hospitalization is twice that of non-poor children, and their average total hospital days are four times that of children in higher social classes (Eqbuono and Starfield, 1982). Poverty places children in double jeopardy because they are more likely to be ill and they are more likely to suffer continuing consequences from these conditions (Starfield, 1982). The length of time a child lives in poverty must inevitably have an important bearing on outcome. The next figure shows expected years of poverty as a function of various family characteristics (U.S. Congress, 1985).

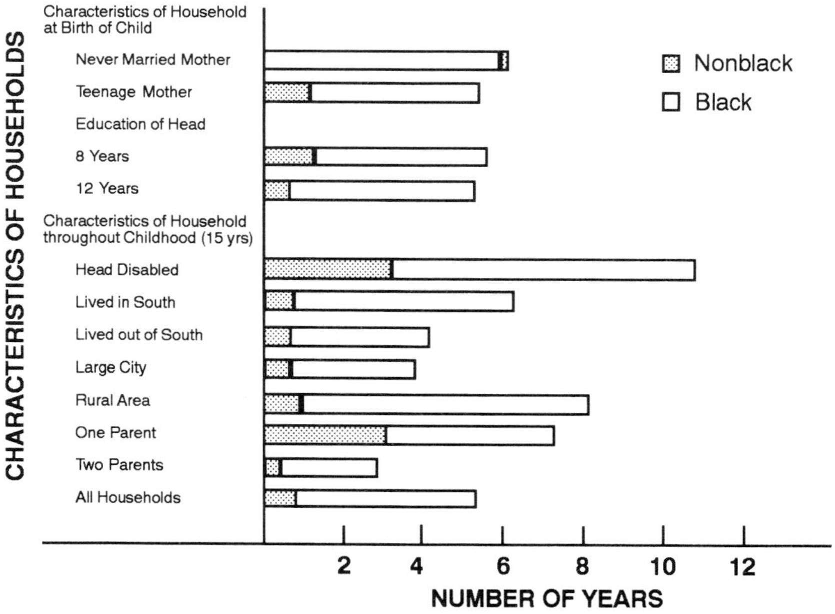

Figure 10
Expected years of childhood poverty out of first 15 years of life for the year 1984. [Source of statistical data: Children in Poverty (Report No. WMCP-99-8), May 22, 1985, Congress of the United States, Washington, DC.].

At this point, an overview of recent socioeconomic trends for the United States would be helpful to provide some insight into the nature of poverty, particularly who is most affected by adverse conditions. The next figure shows the percentage change over time by race, age and family characteristics.

Although these statistics pertain to the United States, economic conditions have been worsening throughout many of the Western industrialized nations. These data should have relevance for other countries. From 1979 through 1984 there has been a 23% increase for people falling below the poverty level. In 1984, 34% of women who headed household with no husband, lived in poverty, along with 16% of white children and 46% of black children under 18 years of age. Today, in 1987, there are approximately 37 million poor people in the United States. Over the past 10 years we have experienced a steady negative change with respect to poverty rates, as these increases have occurred among women and children, especially children. Some of these facts are graphically displayed in Figure 12.

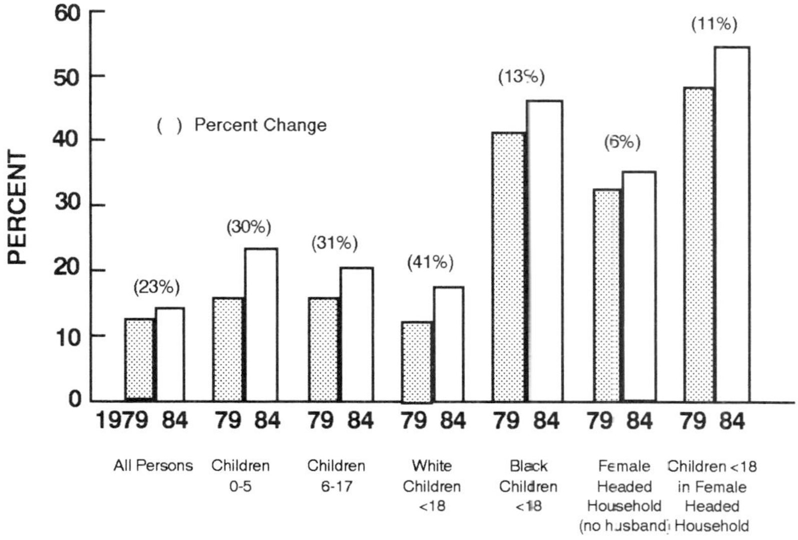

Figure 11
Percentage of population below poverty level by selected characteristics, 1979 and 1984. (Source of statistical data: Statistical Abstract of the United States, 1986, Bureau of the Census Bureau, Washington, DC; and A Children's Defense Budget, Children's Defense Fund, 1986, Washington, DC.)

For children 6 through 17 years old, the poverty rate since 1975 has risen from 16.2% to 19.7% in 1984, amounting to a 21.6% increase over the past 10 years. Children 1 through 5 years of age have seen an increase of 27% over the same period of time (18.4% to 23.4%), and this represents the highest rate for any single group of individuals

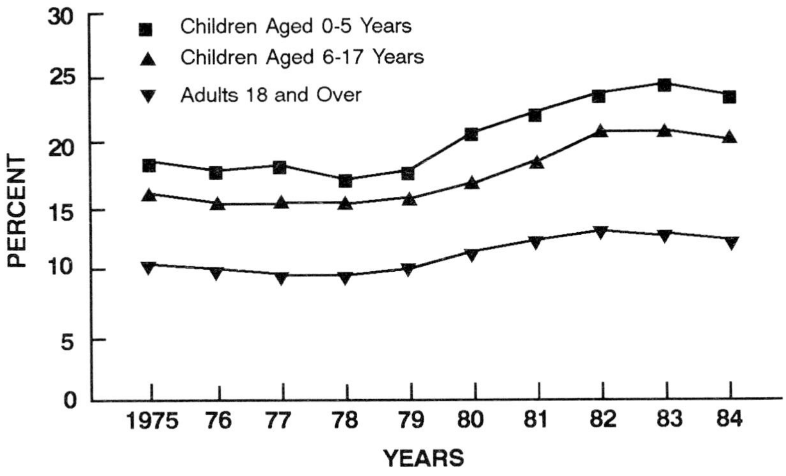

Figure 12
Poverty rates by age group, 1975-1984. (Source: A Children's Defense Budget, Children's Defense Fund, 1986, Washington, DC.)

Data on social class and its relationship to preterm birth and low birthweight are relatively sparse in the United States, owing to the lack of information concerning income and occupation on birth records. However, there are good data from the United Kingdom where social class has been used as a measure for years in different studies of pregnancy outcome. These studies show that poverty has been found to be a major risk factor for low birthweight and preterm birth (Fedrick and Anderson, 1976; Fedrick and Adelstein, 1978).

In the book *Inequalities in Health: The Black Report,* Black et al.(1982) state that health, and to a large extent, survival, is determined very strongly by social factors. A salient case in point is the relationship between social class and childhood accidents, the main cause of mortality for children ages 1 through 14 years of age. They report that risk of being struck by an automobile and dying is five times greater for children in social classes 4 and 5, than in social class 1, and the disparity is even greater for other accidental causes of death such as fire, falls and drownings. A social class tendency can be found for almost all of the adverse factors known to cause poor health.

In a recent study conducted in Montreal, Canada, pertaining to accidents and injuries among children, it was shown that pedestrian and bicycle injuries in low income areas were four to nine times greater than those in more affluent areas (Pless et al.,1987). A similar study in Tennessee, again, revealed a much higher rate of injuries among poor children, one-half of whom lived in female-headed households (Rivara and Barber, 1985).

The second subgrouping under Predisposing Variables is what we call behavioral factors. These include alcohol and tobacco use, nutrition and prenatal care.

Smoking and alcohol. In 1979 our Surgeon General concluded that smoking slows fetal growth, doubles the chance of low birthweight, and increases the risk of stillbirth. Since 1957 more than 50 studies have been conducted involving more than 500,000 births from various ethnic groups and nationalities on the effects of smoking on birthweight. Smoking during pregnancy reduces birthweight by 150-250 grams, retards intrauterine growth, and decreases gestation by 1-2 days. These findings are significant in view of the fact that between 20-30 percent of pregnant women in the United States smoke (Institute of Medicine, 1985).

Fetal Alcohol Syndrome has been recognized as a major cause of congenital malformations and neurologic handicaps. Incidence in the U.S. is about 1-2 per 1,000 live births, and from 30-40% among infants of alcoholic mothers. Alcohol consumption is on the increase among certain groups, particularly among young women, an especially unfortunate correlation (Select Committee on Children, Youth and Families, 1983; AAUAP, 1984; NICHHD, 1985).

Nutrition. Recent findings by the National Center for Health Statistics have shown that maternal weight gain is extremely important to the health of the infant. Women who gained less than 21 lbs. during their pregnancy were more than twice as likely to deliver a LBW infant than those women who gained more. This was true even when factors such as age, education, birth order, and period of gestation were controlled. From this same study the National Center for Health Statistics also found that adequate weight gain could reduce fetal deaths by 40-59%, depending on length of gestation or pregnancy (American Public Health Association, 1986). Again, the irony is such that women who are at higher risk for pregnancy problems are the ones who are least likely to have adequate weight gain. Black women, teens, low income women, and women who smoke or drink are among these.

Prenatal care. Prenatal care is an important consideration influencing the outcome of pregnancy, yet many disadvantaged women in the U.S. do not receive this attention. Numerous potential health problems can be detected during the first visit. The Institute of Medicine has concluded that high quality prenatal care initiated in the first trimester can be a major determinant in reducing incidence of low birthweight as well as other undesirable outcomes. Virtually all studies we have reviewed indicate that prenatal care is most effective in reducing risk of low birthweight among high risk women, whether the risk derives from medical factors, sociodemographic factors, or both.

The third subgroup under Predisposing Variables includes genetic and biological factors. Space does not permit extended discussion of these conditions but they include abnormalities of chromosome structure or number. The three most common chromosomal disorders responsible for maldevelopment of the nervous system include Down's syndrome, sex chromosome disorders and the Fragile X syndrome (NICHHD, 1985).

All predisposing variables whether demographic, behavioral, or genetic, are known to have possible causal links with increased prenatal problems, preterm birth, low birthweight, and intrauterine growth retardation. These proximal variables are, in turn, closely associated with increased morbidity, especially neurodevelopmental and health problems. We shall focus on probably the most important proximal variable - low birthweight. We have already dealt with some descriptive aspects of this major developmental problem.

There were approximately 253,554 low birthweight infants in the United States in 1985 comprising 6.8% of the total (National Center for Health Statistics, 1987). A LBW infant is 40 times more likely to die in the first 4 weeks of life than a normal weight infant (Institute of Medicine, 1985). For those infants weighing less than 1,500 grams there is a four-fold increase that they will be rehospitalized during their first year of life when compared with infants weighing over 2,500 grams. If they do survive, LBW infants are three times more likely to present neurodevelopmental handicaps, and this risk increases as birthweight decreases. They are also at a significantly greater risk of developing such long-term disabilities as cerebral palsy, autism, mental retardation, vision and hearing impairments, school failure and affective disorders (Children's Defense Fund, 1986d). The Institute of Medicine estimates that between 8-19% of very low birthweight infants may be severely affected. It appears that other long-term developmental problems, particularly learning disabilities are more common among children who were low birthweight especially at the mid-range (K.G. Scott, personal communication, March 25, 1987). Boldman and Reed (1976) reviewed incidence data for low birthweight in 21 countries. Per capita income was the best indicator for LBW. Despite genetic variability, the crucial factors associated with LBW are environmental. Comparative data are displayed in Figure 13.

On considering those most likely to give birth to a LBW infant in the United States, a pattern can be discerned. Demographically, those at highest risk are under 17 and over 34 years, black, low SES, unmarried, and have a low level of education. Behavioural and environmental risks include smoking, poor nutritional status, substance abuse, and toxic exposures including occupational hazards.

PERCENTAGE OF LOW BIRTHWEIGHT LIVE BIRTHS
IN SELECTED DEVELOPED COUNTRIES — 1980

1.	Norway	3.25
2.	Sweden	4.03
3.	Switzerland	5.14
4.	Japan	5.18
5.	New Zealand	5.27
6.	Federal Republic of Germany	5.51
7.	Austria	5.68
8.	Denmark	6.00
9.	Canada	6.10
10.	German Democratic Republic	6.19
11.	Italy	6.71
12.	Scotland	6.73
13.	United Kingdom (England/Wales)	6.79
14.	United States	6.84
15.	Israel	7.16

Figure 13
Percentage of low birthweight live births in selected developed countries - 1980. (Source: Preventing Low Birthweight, Institute of Medicine, Washington, DC.: National Academy Press, 1985).

Health care risks include absent or inadequate prenatal care, and iatrogenic prematurity (Institute of Medicine, 1985). Two articles in the British *Journal of Obstetrics and Gynaecology*, pertaining to poor pregnancy outcome, reported that when social classes I and II were compared with classes IV and V, the rate of spontaneous preterm births was 50% greater in the lower two classes. In the second study, dealing with delivering LBW infants at term, the rates in social classes IV and V were 70% greater than those in social classes I and II (Fedrick and Adelstein, 1978; Fedrick and Anderson, 1986).

Up to this point we have discussed outcome variables, predisposing variables and proximal variables. Two other sets of variables that are highly correlated with and may in fact have possible causal links with morbidity are those of poverty and limited resources. While much has been said concerning SES, it is important to expand upon the topic of poverty and its connection to morbidity.

Poverty, whether chronic or acute, can affect the individual in both subtle and profound ways, impacting negatively on intellectual, emotional, and physical development. Perhaps it should go without saying that poverty makes the environment less conducive to optimal development, whether from poor nutrition, inadequate medical care, parental absence or neglect, reduced opportunity for schooling, etc. It is important to view poverty not as an isolated or singular condition, but rather as ongoing processes affecting all developmental levels. There are three major ways in which social, cultural and economic factors contribute to brain disorders (Avery, 1985).

1. During gestation and after birth disadvantaged children who are reared under adverse circumstances that cause damage to the brain.

2. For those who have suffered central nervous system injury, lack of quick access to effective habilitative services may permanently impair development during a critical period. (We understand, of course, that not everyone accepts the "critical period" notion).

3. Children who are brain injured and who are reared in an unfavorable environment may be placed in double jeopardy in that the poor adaptive outcome may be compounded by the combination of these two factors averaged together.

While poverty is correlated with many of the predisposing and outcome variables, there is little doubt that poverty is the major catalyst behind the inability of an individual to access many resources that, if utilized, could have profound results for health, welfare and development. These resources consist of factors that allow individuals to take control of their lives by exercising options available to them, and having the ability to make responsible choices. Resource variables include but are not limited to pregnancy, contraceptive and venereal disease counselling; classes in proper nutrition and child care; free prenatal care; free quality day care for children of mothers who work or want to go back to school; vocational skill classes; family and child abuse counselling; and child and adolescent mental health facilities to name a few. Such resources and opportunities should be available in every community, and should occupy high priority when budget allocations are being made on all levels. All too often, these services and options are limited, and when available, are often difficult to access, crowded, and much of the time understaffed. Also, the very individuals who could derive the greatest benefit from these resources are those most likely who, for any number of reasons, poverty not being the least, cannot take full advantage, and thus suffer the most adverse consequences.

In one of our studies we have found evidence of a fairly direct connection between poverty level and birth outcomes. The current income level in the U.S. that defines family poverty is $10,900. The 50 states vary in terms of how much they supplement poor families to bring them up to this level. We gathered data on each and correlated the average supplement with low birthweight and infant mortality. The correlations between monthly poverty level and low birthweight were -.50 and -.35 for whites and blacks, respectively. The correlations between monthly poverty level and postneonatal mortality and infant mortality were -.45 and -.40 respectively. The overall relationship is clear; its sources are more difficult to disentangle.

While poverty cannot be singled out as the only factor having a deleterious influence on health and development, there is evidence showing beyond any doubt that children who are subjected to social disadvantage, limited resources, and the accompanying environmental stress associated with substandard living conditions are more susceptible to, and suffer from inordinate rates of illness, disability, and injuries when compared with those who are more affluent.

SUMMARY

By way of summary, problems associated with the New Morbidity are complex and profound in their effect on individuals and society. Costs both in human and economic terms far outweigh investments of time and resources in research, treatment and prevention. As societies become more complex and pressured, and as more families face economic hardships, our children will undoubtedly become the victims of many new psychosocial, developmental and behavioral stresses. The problems are complex; the solutions no less.

The relatively high risk of the New Morbidity, including mental retardation, among poor people and those in lower SES groups is best characterized by a transactional process in which certain children are behaviourally and biologically vulnerable to environmental and social variations predisposing them to an array of disabling conditions. The connection between poverty and mental retardation is not direct, but is mediated by a host of proximal and distal variables. The truth is that our knowledge of the precise nature of the correlations, and these causes and effects, is imperfect. But we do know enough about some of these conditions to intervene preventively in ways that improve quality of life and that are cost effective.

Let us suggest that poverty is not good for children. And here, in summary, are some considerations, not all of which are entirely new (e.g., Birch and Gussow, 1970). In fact, in 1912 the U.S. Children's Bureau identified some of these potential problems. The environments in which economically disadvantaged children develop are less conducive to good physical, mental and behavioral development than the environments of children not disadvantaged. These differences are deep rooted, fundamental, enduring and intergenerational, facts that have not received sufficient respect. As children themselves mothers of disadvantaged children are not so well nourished, they are smaller, and they receive less nurturing care. As a group when of childbearing age, they have children younger (frequently as teenagers), more rapidly, more often, and they continue to bear them to an older age. When such a mother is pregnant her general health will be poorer than that of a woman who is better off, her fetus faces greater risk of infection, intoxication, and trauma. Prenatal and general health care are less accessible to her. She is more likely to deliver her child under substandard conditions. Children of such mothers, on the average, are smaller for gestational age, are more likely to be premature, die more readily and suddenly, are sicker in infancy, suffer a greater rate of accidents, and run a greater risk of neglect than children born into better circumstances. Surviving the first few weeks of life, their mortality thereafter is excessively high, their illnesses more frequent, more persistent and more severe. Development is negatively influenced by the mother's health, age, income level, education and habits. During school years, children's nutrition may be inadequate, they miss more school more frequently, their housing is frequently substandard, family income is low, and family disorganization is high. They will present a higher rate of learning problems, behaviour disturbances, allergies, and speech difficulties (Freeman, 1985).

Disadvantage, whether economic, education, or biologic, occurs through time, each generation passing on to the next the unfortunate and cumulative consequences of its own experience, as in any ever enlarging circle, with no clear beginning and no clear end. Neither the much rehearsed cultural-deficit nor the vulnerable genetic-inheritance theory is adequate to explain the development of different forms of social competence, economic inequality, and biologic vulnerability. However, there are more sophisticated, albeit complex, developmental models that could form the basis for policy-oriented prevention of some pathology associated with the New Morbidity (Laosa, 1979).

A great deal of data support the foregoing conclusions. And what of technology? We can expect many scientific and technical advances including new tests, new drugs, new genetic engineering breakthroughs. But, will technology solve our problem and propel us to the 50% goal? We submit that the kinds of solutions and interventions needed are not primarily of a technological nature, but are more of social/political nature. Of course, research and technology will have a great deal to contribute to our understanding of the problems we face and we should use that technology for all that it is worth. But we should not be misled into thinking that science by itself will solve those problems. We must not permit ourselves to be confounded by a futurism that forces commitment of ends to new and more convenient means. More than ever we need to focus attention on fundamental ethical and moral issues that attend to the problem of developmental disabilities and our society at large.

INTERVENTION AND PREVENTION: RECOMMENDATIONS

While basic medical science plays a significant role in the amelioration of mental retardation and other developmental disabilities, especially in light of new discoveries concerning genetic components, it would be an error to assume that all answers lie within the parameters of biomedical disciplines. Too often we are taken by new 'Starwar' discoveries and interventions, at the expense of ignoring less spectacular but more cost effective long-term solutions.

A case in point is that of low birthweight infants. While thousands of babies have been saved by heroic medical interventions within the NICUs, there is another side to the story. At the same time these babies are being saved, their chances of exhibiting signs of later developmental and neurological delay are greatly increased, especially for those under 1,500 grams. Also the economic costs to parents and society are enormous and growing. This is not to say that these medical measures should not be taken; on the contrary, we should use every resource available to intervene for the purpose of saving and improving lives. However, when less expensive and invasive prevention strategies are available and known to be effective, it is imperative that we utilize them. Figure 14 displays a list of prevention alternatives.

Just as the problems they address stem from many different factors, intervention and prevention strategies must take a multifaceted approach if they are to be effective. This approach includes the input of medicine and the related technologies, education, and social/political programs, all making a concerted and coordinated effort to discover solutions to these problems.

An important area to which we can direct our attention is that of teenage pregnancy. While teen pregnancy in the U.S. has declined by almost 25% from 1970-1983, the number of unmarried teens giving birth has increased by almost 33% during the same period of time. In 1983, 53% of teenage births were to unmarried mothers (Children's Defense Fund, 1986b). There is nothing medicine can do to prevent teen pregnancy until after the fact and then in the heat of controversy. However, education and social programs can play a vital role if we are willing to address the problem in our schools and communities. Programs on sexuality, pregnancy, and contracep-

SELECTED FACTORS IN PREVENTION

I. **SOCIOECONOMIC/ENVIRONMENTAL**
Nutrition: WIC, AFDC, Food Stamp Programs
Medical Care: Access to rural and inner-city populations
Sanitation: Improve plumbing, control rodents/pests
Safety: Improve lighting, playgrounds, traffic control
Teratogens/Poisoning: Awareness and avoidance

II. **PRENATAL/PERINATAL/POSTNATAL**
Access to adequate and timely prenatal care
Medical intervention in preterm birth
Ensure safe labor and delivery
Follow-up services for mother and infants
Identification/intervention for high risk infants

III. **EDUCATIONAL**
Teen pregnancy, contraception, VD programs
Genetic counseling
Family planning clinics

IV. **PERSONAL/BEHAVIORAL**
Substance abuse counseling
Child abuse counseling
Techniques for reducing stress
Access to adolescent mental health clinics

Figure 14
Selected Factors in the prevention of infant and child morbidity and mortality.

tion should be offered as part of the school curriculum. Family planning clinics should be available in every community and be easily accessible to anyone in need of or desiring such services. Government agencies at all levels must also become involved in education and awareness campaigns.

Prenatal care is known to be effective in reducing infant morbidity and mortality, if it is timely and adequate. In fact, data presented to the U.S. Congress recently has shown that free prenatal care would be a highly cost-effective prevention measure. Government should provide resources to communities to ensure that every pregnant woman receives free prenatal care starting in the critical first trimester.

Two very important personal behaviours that adversely affect the growing fetus and that can result in LBW and a vast array of physical and mental disabilities are smoking and alcohol consumption.

While perhaps not as dramatic as alcohol, smoking has been linked with LBW, which in turn, is associated with higher morbidity and mortality. Alcohol, on the other hand, can cause Fetal Alcohol Syndrome. These are totally preventable outcomes. We must continue to make people aware of the dangers associated with this behaviour, and again there is probably no better place to start than in our schools. The media should also play a crucial role in informing the public, in an effective manner, of these health facts. Of particular importance is the creation of a network of community-based clinics and counseling centers.

Poverty, while not an independent factor in morbidity, nonetheless acts as a proxy for so many of the variables that, in turn, increase the risk of disability. Inadequate prenatal care, single teenage pregnancy, poor nutrition, and low educational attainment, while not exclusive to any one segment of society, are more readily encountered among the poor. While poverty can touch anyone, the largest and fastest growing groups finding themselves among the ranks of the poor are those of women and children. After the child is born, the environment he/she grows up in can have a profound influence on cognition, physical and psychosocial development. Environmental stress, inadequate medical care, and the possibility of emotional and physical abuse, are all exasperated in socially disadvantaged environments.

CONCLUSION

The picture we have painted in this brief account is not particularly encouraging in many respects. As we examine the data describing the New Morbidity, and as we begin to disentangle the many contributing causes and correlations, at several different levels of analysis, we also gain a new respect for the complexity of the problems that we seek to address. What should be clear, however is that, these are not insoluble problems, complex and intricate as they may be. What is evident from this analysis is that the scientific, social, economic, and political response must recognise these complexities. And that simple, one-time, inexpensive and univariate solutions will not be effective. If the constellation of problems is complex, our response can be no less.

We do have models, the techniques, the scientific knowledge base, and the resources to prevent many childhood morbidities. But all this will avail of us little without the resolve to meet the challenge of the future, for the future is the children.

REFERENCES

American Association of University Affiliated Programs forPersons with Developmental Disabilities (1984) *Developmental handicaps: Prevention and Treatment* **II** (pp. 26-34). Silver Springs, MD:.

American Public Health Association (1986) Correlations underscored: Maternal weight gain, infant birth weight. *The Nation's Health.* pp. 1-6.

Avery, G. (1985) Effects of social, cultural and economicfactors on brain development. In J.M. Freeman (Ed.) *Prenatal and perinatal factors associated with brain disorders* (pp. 163-164). NIH Publication No. 85-1149. Bethesda, MD: National Institutes of Health.

Barth, R.P. (1986) *Social and cognitive treatment of children and adolescents.* San Francisco: Jossey-Bass.

Baumeister, A.A. (1981) Mental retardation policy and research:The unfulfilled promise. *American Journal of Mental Deficiency,* **85,** 449- 456.

Baumeister, A.A. & Hamlett, C.L. (1986) A National Survey of State-Sponsored Programs to Prevent Fetal Alcohol Syndrome. *Mental Retardation,* **24,** 169-173.

Baumeister, A.A. & MacLean, W.E., Jr. (1979) Brain damage andmental retardation. In N.R. Ellis (Ed.) *Handbook of mental deficiency: Psychological theory and research.* Hillsdale, NJ: L. Erlbaum Assoc.

Berg, J.M. (1986) Physical determinants of environmental origin. In A.M. Clarke, A.D.B. Clarke & J.M. Berg (Eds.) *Mental deficiency: The changing outlook.* New York: The Free Press.

Birch, H. G. & Gussow, J.D. (1970) *Disadvantaged Children: Health, Nutrition and School Failure.* New York: Grune and Stratton.

Binkin, N., Williams, R., Hogue, C. & Chen, P. (1985) Reducing Black neonatal mortality: Will improvement in birth weight be enough? *Journal of the American Medical Association,* **253** (3), 372-375.

Black, D., Morris, J., Smith, C., & Townsend, P. (1982) In P.Townsend & N. Davidson (Eds.) *Inequalities in health: The Black report.* New York: Penguin Books.

Boldman, R., & Reed, D. (1977) Worldwide variations in low birth weight. In D. Reed & F. Harley (Eds.) *The epidemiology of prematurity* (pp. 39-52). Baltimore: Urban & Schwarzenberg Publishers.

Butler, J.A., Starfield, B., & Stenmark, S. (1984) Child health policy. In H.W. Stevenson & A.E. Siegel (Eds.) *Child development research and social policy.* Chicago: The University of Chicago Press.

Children's Defense Fund. (1986a) *Building health programs for teenagers* (pp. 4-12). Washington, DC: Author.

Children's Defense Fund. (1986b) *Welfare and teen pregnancy: What do we know? What do we do?* (pp. 6-7). Washington, DC: Author.

Children's Defense Fund (1986c) *A children's defense budget: An analysis of the FY 1987 federal budget and children.* Washington, DC: Author.

Children's Defense Fund (1986d) *Maternal and child health databook: The health of America's children.* Washington, DC: Author.

Clarke, A.D.B., & Clarke, A.M. (1977) Prospects for preventionand amelioration of mental retardation: a guest editorial. *American Journal of Mental Deficiency,* **81,** 523-533.

Eqbuono, L. & Starfield, B. (1982) Child health and social status. *Pediatrics,* **69** (5), 550-557.

Fedrick, J., & Adelstein, P. (1978) Factors associated with lowbirth weight of infants delivered at term. *British Journal of Obstetrics and Gynaecology*, **85** (1) 1-7.

Fedrick, J. & Anderson, A. (1976) Factors associated with spontaneous preterm birth. *British Journal of Obstetrics and Gynaecology*. **83,** 342-350.

Freeman, J.M. (Ed). (1985) *Prenatal and perinatal factors associated with brain disorders*. Washington, DC: U.S. Department of Health and Human Services.

Geronimus, A. (1986) The effects of race, residence, and prenatal care on the relationship of maternal age to neonatal mortality. *American Journal of Public Health*, **76** (12), 1416-1421.

Grossman, H.J. (Ed.) (1983) *Classification in mental retardation*. Washington, DC: American Association on Mental Deficiency.

Haggerty, R.J., Roughman, K.J. & Pless, I.V. (Eds) (1975) *Child health and community* (pp. 94- 113). New York: Wiley.

Institute of Medicine (1985) *Preventing low birthweight. Washington,* DC: National Academy Press.

Laosa, L.M. (1984) Social policies toward children of diverseethnic, racial, and language groups in the United States. In H.W. Stevenson & A.E. Siegel (Eds.) *Child development research and social policy*. Chicago: University of Chicago Press.

Makinson, C. (1985) *The health consequences of teenage fertility: Family planning perspectives*, **17** (3), 132-139.

National Center for Health Statistics. (1984) *Vital statistics of United States*. Annual summary of births, deaths, marriages and divorces. Washington, DC: U.S. Government Printing Office.

National Center for Health Statistics (1985) *Health United States 1985* (DHSS Publication No. PHS 86-1232). Washington, DC: U.S. Government Printing Office.

National Center for Health Statistics (1986a) *Utilization of short-stay hospitals by diagnosis-relatedgroups*. (DHSS Publication No. PHS 96-1748). Washington, DC: U.S. Government Printing Office.

National Center for Health Statistics (1986b) *Current estimates from the National Health Interview Survey* (DHHS Publication No. 86-1582). Washington, DC: U.S. Government Printing Office.

National Center for Health Statistics (1987) *Advance report of final natality statistics*. Monthly Vital Statistics Report, **36** (DHHS Publication No. PHS 878-1120). Hyattsville, MD: Public Health Service.

National Institute of Child Health and Human Development (1985) *Prenatal and perinatal factors associated with brain disorders* (Publication No. 85-1149) (pp. 121-176). Washington, DC: U.S. Department of Health and Human Services, Public Health Service, NIH.

National Institute of Child Health and Human Development (1986) *An evaluation and assessment of the state of the science: Report of the study group on mental retardation and developmental disabilities* (pp. 37-119). Washington, DC: U.S. Department of Health and Human Services.

Pless, I., Verreault, R., Arsenault, L., Frappier, J. & Stulginskas, J. (1987) The epidemiology of Road accidents in childhood. *American Journal of Public Health*, **77** (3), 358-360

Rivara, F. & Barber, M. (1985) Demographic analysis of childhood pedestrian injuries. *Pediatrics*, **76** (3), 375-381.

Select Committee on Children, Youth and Families (1983) *Prevention strategies for healthy babies and healthy children*. Hearing before the Select Committee on Children, Youth and Families, House of Representatives, 98th Congress. Washington, DC: U.S. Government Printing Office.

Shiono, P. & Klebanoff, M. (1986) Ethnic differences in preterm and very preterm delivery. *American Journal of Public Health,* **76** (11), 1317-1321.

Shiono, P., Klebanoff, M. Graubard, B., Berendes H., & Rhoads, G. (1986) Birth weight among women of different ethnic groups. *Journal of the American Medical Association,* **255** (1), 48-52.

Starfield, B. (1982) Family income, ill health, and medical care of U.S. children. *Journal of Public Health Policy,* **3** (3), 244- 259.

United States Congress (1985) *Children in poverty,* (Report No.WMCP-99-8)., Washington DC.: U.S. Government Printing Office.

Wilson, R.S. (1983) The Lousiville twin study: Developmental synchronies in behaviour. *Child Development,* **54,** 298-316.

Wilson, R.S. (1985) Risk and resilience in early mental development. *Developmental Psychology,* **21,** 795-805.

Zigler, E. (1978) National crisis in mental retardation. *American Journal of Mental Deficiency,* **83,** 1-8.

Zigler, E., Balla, D. & Hodapp, R. (1984) On the definition and classification of mental retardation. *American Journal of Mental Deficiency,* **89,** 215-230.

CHAPTER 6

Thirty Years of Education for Pupils With Moderate Learning Difficulties

Ronald Gulliford

Department of Special Education, University of Birmingham, UK

INTRODUCTION

The problem of educating the small group of children with the greatest difficulty in learning became obvious when school attendance was made compulsory in 1880. By the turn of the century, the first special classes had been set up in urban areas. Provision was made mandatory by the 1914 Act; children had to be certified by a doctor as feeble minded before placement. The 1945 Handicapped Pupils and School Health Service Regulations after the 1944 Act reflected the findings of the Wood Report (1929) that some 10% of school children were educationally retarded. They were defined as pupils "who by reason of limited ability or other conditions resulting in educational retardation require some specialized form of education wholly or partly in substitution for the education normally given in ordinary schools." In spite of the unfortunate term *educationally subnormal*, (ESN) the new approach stimulated placement of a continually increasing number of children in special schools for the ESN and a broader interpretation of the need for special school placement. The intention of making more and better arrangements for backward children in ordinary schools was only partly achieved during the 30 years under review. While special schools were able to develop a more or less distinctive curricular approach, provision in ordinary schools showed considerable uncertainty about curricular aims, objectives and methods.

MODERATE LEARNING DIFFICULTIES

The term "moderate learning difficulties" was first used in the Warnock Report - significantly in a chapter entitled "Some curricular issues" - and distinguished severe, moderate, mild and specific learning difficulties. Following implementation of the 1981 Act in 1983, a statistical return required pupils in special schools to be recorded according to their need for one of three types of curriculum. Those with mild difficulties are deemed to need a mainstream curriculum with support; those with moderate difficulties need a modified curriculum which should be similar to a mainstream curriculum but while not limited in its expectations, has objectives more appropriate to children whose needs would not properly be met by a mainstream curriculum. Those with severe learning difficulties need a developmental curriculum providing a range of educational experiences with particular attention to personal autonomy and social skills and to well defined objectives.

The change in terminology should not be seen as just a new label. Whereas the 1945 definition referred to "some specialized form of education *wholly or partly in substitution* for the education normally given", the 1983 description refers to a curriculum *similar to a mainstream curriculum* with appropriate objectives though not restricted in its expectations. Put simply, the difference is that whereas much publication and practice in the education of ESN children was concerned with the aims and nature of a *special* curriculum, the post-1981 curriculum should be a *modified mainstream* one. This may appear unrealistic but it can be justified in terms of *educational aims* and in the light of current *developments* in *practice* whereby ordinary schools are trying to improve access to the curriculum and special schools are looking for closer links with mainstream schools.

Strictly, therefore, we cannot speak of 30 years of education for pupils with moderate learning difficulties but only four since 1983, plus 26 years of education for pupils termed educationally subnormal.

Looking back 30 years takes us to 1957 in which year there were 27,000 pupils in special schools for the educationally subnormal. This was a remarkable change from pre-war. Between 1914 and 1938 the number of feeble minded children in special schools had only risen from 13,000 in 1914 to 18,000 in 1938, dropping to 11,000 in 1946. In spite of the unfortunate term, *educationally subnormal,* the post-war changes led to a considerable expansion of special school provision, schools being established in small towns and rural areas where previously there had been none. The numbers of pupils continued to increase until it was over 50,000 in the early 1980s.

Whereas pre-war school medical officers were reluctant to recommend special school placement for IQs above 70, the broader definition of educationally subnormal and the involvement of educational psychologists in ascertainment procedures led to broader criteria for placement. Williams and Gruber (1967) found that 45% of their sample in special schools in South Wales had IQs over 70;

Rutter et al. (1970) found a quarter; Marra (1979) 49%. These figures indicate that there must have been - and still are - many children with very limited ability remaining in ordinary schools. These and other reports provide evidence that pupils in special schools tended to have a combination of difficulties in speech and language, minor physical and sensory disabilities, emotional and behaviour difficulties and were more frequently from social classes IV and V. Rutter et. al. (1970, Table 9,3) show that special school placement on the Isle of Wight was determined by severity of educational handicap as much as intellectual retardation.

The Ministry did refer several times to the needs of the 10% of retarded pupils in ordinary schools. In 1946, Pamphlet No. 5 said: "The problem of finding a way of educating them is one which the modern school must face and the staff will be justified in trying out enterprising methods and organization. It is of outstanding importance that such pupils should not be entirely segregated from their fellows and from the corporate life of the school and that whatever course of work they follow it should have a real purpose and meaning for them..... There is room here for much thought and experiment. "(Ministry of Education, 1946). These integrationist sentiments were echoed in a Cheshire Education Committee publication in 1956. They were not in favour of special schools and classes for dull children (IQ 55-85) and stated that "the liberal aims of modern education with its emphasis on the total personality rather than limited training in certain skills cannot adequately be met in special schools or classes which provide artificial social conditions even more remote from the ordinary world than the normal school". The committee advocated integration, mixed ability teaching, good record keeping and the early involvement of parents. It is curious that the Warnock Report in 1978 was thought to be proposing new ideas!

In 1961 a Ministry circular gave a reminder about provision in ordinary schools and itemized three ways:

i) employment of suitable peripatetic teachers to advise and assist ordinary schools to provide special educational treatment.

ii) establishment of remedial classes or centres to help temporarily retarded children.

iii) the provision of special classes at selected schools for children drawn from an area of schools.

iv) diagnostic centres for young handicapped children.

i) Services of *peripatetic remedial teachers* had begun to develop during the 1950's, mostly withdrawing children in school or into remedial education centres. Surveys of age groups enabled them to select children for remedial help, which tended to exclude children considered more appropriately placed in special schools or classes. But research cast doubt about the long-term effects of remedial teaching and there were also always more children needing help than could be given it. The remedial teachers' role changed towards advisory and in-service training work with teachers. In the 1970s, following the Bullock and Warnock Reports, they began to see their status as a service supporting teachers in providing for retarded children in the classroom; their interests and concerns broadened to remedial work across the curriculum, not just basic skills. A specialist teaching role remains in respect of children with specific learning difficulties.

A similar support role was suggested for special schools in the Warnock Report. A well known example was at a newly established school at Peterborough which, having developed its curriculum and associated resources, offered the help of an out-reach teacher to some adjacent primary schools (Hallmark and Dessent, 1982). The source of the scheme was said to be the School Psychological Services, disenchantment with segregation and with the arbitrary division of children into ESN or remedial. They saw learning difficulties as forming a continuum of need requiring a continuum of provision. Breaking down the insularity of special schooling and developing links between ordinary and special schools would encourage return of children to mainstream. The visiting teacher visited primary schools once a week (similar to the Portage model) and in liaison with the class teacher formulated programmes of work for the selected pupils - and also provided appropriate learning materials. It proved an effective form of in-service training for teachers. It was also effective in maintaining retarded pupils in the ordinary school and facilitated the return of some pupils from special school. A recent enquiry by the NFER found that 74 per cent of 268 special schools had cooperative links with ordinary schools; the nature and quality of these links, however, were very variable.

Outreach teaching or a support service provided by special schools has potential. But reports indicate that the scheme needs to be well-planned, that the support teachers should have something to offer, that conditions are favourable in the receiving school and that the scheme is well-resourced with staff time and is adequately monitored. In a time of falling rolls it has been seen as a desirable development in many special schools. In some cases, children from ordinary schools have even been placed in a special school for a term or more - a contrast to the previous reluctance to place children in special schools.

ii) *Special classes* for the most backward children were no new thing during this period but they continued to increase in number. The figures have not always been recorded in education statistics.

Part-time remedial groups certainly increased in primary schools: surveys for the Bullock Report in 1973 found that two-thirds of primary schools organized remedial reading groups (average size 6) and that 11.9% organized special classes; 19% of schools had a visiting remedial teacher. In a sample of 308 secondary schools the arrangements included: withdrawal (63% of schools); one- term remedial classes (25%); remedial classes or streams (52%). The quality of provision was variable and the Committee was critical of a prolonged emphasis on remedial work with few opportunities for achieving success in other activities and also concluded that, in many secondary schools, work with slow learners ranked low in the list of priorities. The Bullock Report's conclusions echoed the findings of a DES survey of slow learners in secondary schools in 1971: uncertainty of aims, objectives and methods; the negative effects of streaming; exposure to inappropriate specialist subject teaching; lack of status for the teachers concerned with slow learners. It was concluded that "there is much to be done before the needs of slow learners in secondary schools can be satisfactorily met".

It is no wonder that during the last 30 years the number of retarded children placed in special schools increased to a peak at age 14:- in 1983 there were 2,385 seven year olds, but over 7,364 at 14. Nor is it surprising that there is little evidence of transfer of ESN pupils back to ordinary schools. Fleeman (1984) was able to get information about 33 pupils from three Birmingham special schools who, over a 7 year period, were transferred around age 13. Transfer was judged successful in 20% (some getting some CSE passes); 50% made a moderate adjustment; 30% unsuccessful.

One has to recognize, however, that secondary schools have been continuously meeting new situations and demands: the post-war shortage of teachers; the school leaving age raised twice, 1948 and 1973; reorganization on comprehensive school lines (there were 262 in 1965; 1000 in 1970; 3000 in 1975). In many areas, ethnic minority groups were being assimilated and much effort went into teaching English as a second language.

In recent years, there has been a greater awareness of the negative effects of streaming and special grouping. The concept and practice of support teaching within classes of mixed ability has been developing in secondary schools, in some cases with well-organized systems of support for pupils with special needs and for their teachers. More will be said about this later.

iii) The third suggestion in the 1961 Circular was "the provision of *special classes at selected schools* for children drawn from an area of schools". There have always been examples of these, particularly in rural areas, as a means of avoiding long travelling distances to special schools or as an alternative to residential special schooling. In 1983,

DES statistics recorded that 8203 pupils were attending designated-special classes in primary and secondary schools. In Wales in 1979, about 9000 pupils were recorded as educationally subnormal, nearly five thousand of whom were in special classes. An HMI report, (Welsh Office, 1984) provides a view of 13 primary units (37 classes) in Gwent catering for 334 pupils. Three-quarters of the pupils had IQs below 80. The general impression was of a satisfactory educational provision which was welcomed by the host schools - except for "a reluctance on the part of mainstream teachers to accept responsibility for children from the special classes" and sometimes a reluctance of headteachers to risk disrupting mainstream work by integrative movement of pupils. Similar findings were reported by Lowden (1984) from a study of 53 units in Wales. Although the attitudes of teachers and parents towards provision for retarded children in ordinary primary schools were very favourable in principle this was not so manifest in practice. There was little active effort to bring about integration; more than half of the ordinary class teachers expressed a preference not to have children from the Units integrated in their classes.

For a number of reasons - financial; falling rolls in special schools; the integration philosophy - it seems likely that there may be more, and more varied, provisions in ordinary schools for children with moderate learning difficulties. There are already some which aspire to provide opportunities for curricular as well as social integration. There are examples of outreach teachers working from special schools; and classes in ordinary schools taught by teachers from the special school; special teachers providing support in one or a number of schools. We need more evaluation of such schemes as well as the strategies which the ordinary primary teacher uses. It is commonly assumed that the primary class teacher is experienced in organizing special help to children with marked special needs. How they could be further advised on that management task is a matter meriting further study.

There is also a need for further study of support teaching. Should the support teacher concentrate on the pupil with marked special needs or give help to others? How far should it be seen as collaborative teaching involving cooperation in planning the lesson? What are the inter-personal problems of two teachers working in the same class? What indeed are the potential difficulties for the support teacher who may miss the enjoyment and achievement of working with class groups over the full range of curriculum?

iv) The Circular in 1961 also suggested the establishment of diagnostic centres especially for young children who appear to be exceptionally handicapped, to help decide the best form of future treatment. This encouraged provision of diagnostic or assessment classes in special schools for children below age 7years. An HMI survey (1970) found that such centres included children with a great variety of difficulties, a large proportion with severe learning difficulties. Speech and language disorders were common. About half went on to ESN school, a quarter to mental handicap centres, and 1 in 10 to primary school. At that time, some 1300 children aged 4 to 6 are recorded as placed in ESN schools. In 1983 there were 2654. Swann (1985) has concluded that statistics show an increase in the proportion of young children in special schools for MLD. Obviously many retarded children of pre- school age will be in ordinary pre-school provision. We should note that several researches show that there is too little involvement by psychologists, speech therapists and advisers in early education assessment and programmes.

DEVELOPMENT OF THE CURRICULUM FOR MLD PUPILS

Thirty years ago special schools were in the early stages of exposure to new ideas about the nature of mental retardation and the possibilities for improvement through well planned learning and experience and higher aspirations for pupils' development. Prior to the 1950s, there were few books on the teaching of ESN pupils. I recall the books on the desk of the head of the first ESN school I worked with: Tredgold and Shuttleworth's texts on mental deficiency; Burt's "The Backward Child", Schonell's books on reading, spelling and arithmetic. The pre-1950s special teaching derived from Seguin, Montessori and a watered down elementary school curriculum. Some may have read Descoeudres (1927) whose approach was influenced by Decroly. Some would have read a book by John Duncan which, influenced by Alexander's work on practical versus verbal intelligence, sought to promote verbal development through practical tasks, e.g. reading instructions to do housecraft, craft tasks or science experiments.

The situation changed with the setting up of the first one year courses at London (1950) and Birmingham (1954). By 1960 there were some 13 courses and many others followed in the next 30 years. I recall that an interviewee for my first course was puzzled about what the students would do for a whole year. "What shall we be doing? Make apparatus?" In fact, the course introduced students to child and educational psychology, environmental influences on intelligence and language; to the work of O'Connor, Tizard and Clarke (Clarke and Clarke, 1958), Gunzburg's work with adolescent subnormals contributed to the concept of a leavers' programme. Piaget's (1952) book on number influenced the development of a number programme. Kirk and Johnson's (1951) book was a basic text. When Tansley and I published a book in 1960 our account reflected all these and also a closer relationship with the ordinary school curriculum in contrast with the rather circumscribed pre-war conceptions about teaching the *educationally subnormal*. Creative work, music and drama, study of the human and natural environment, science and a leavers' programme were discussed in addition to language and maths.

In the next 30 years, there were many influences on the curriculum. I would mention first the opportunities provided by new and well equipped school buildings and the influx of new teachers, many of whom saw opportunities for educational experiment, free from the constraints of ordinary schools. In the 1950s, Strauss and Lehtinen's concept of the brain injured child had attracted interest and in the 1960s Kephart's motor training programme, Frostig's perceptual training, Kirk's psycho-linguistic remediation had considerable influence on special schools. On perhaps firmer ground, the study of language and the development of language programmes in compensatory education focussed attention on the language curriculum - a marked contrast with the pre-war sensory and manual training emphasis.

In the 1960s, curriculum theory began to influence schools, particularly that approach which emphasized the definition of aims, goals and objectives. It was common to find schools engaged on curriculum development. Working parties spent hours discussing their objectives, aiming to produce a grand plan. They benefited from the exercise even though they had not given enough thought to implementation. Brennan (1974) made a useful distinction between elements of the curriculum which need to be learnt to the level of mastery and those to the level of awareness. Ainscow and Tweddle (1979) took this further by referring to the 'closed' curriculum of essential skills in reading, writing, number, motor development and social competence which should be defined as behavioural objectives and learnt to the level of mastery. It provided a structure within which task analysis, precision teaching and monitoring could make learning and teaching effective. The development of work in schools for children with severe learning difficulties, although they were then educationally subnormal (severe), contributed to this.

In the late 1970s, the persuasive influence of HMIs and DES reports have been pushing for a balanced curriculum in schools. At the same time, several trends indicate the need for a closer alignment of the special school curriculum with that in ordinary schools: closer links between ordinary and special schools, including the idea of special schools as resource centres; the desirability of special schools distinguishing a secondary curriculum from a primary - in some cases, by separate primary and secondary schools.

DES publications have prompted consideration of nine areas of experience: aesthetic/creative, ethical, linguistic, mathematical, physical, scientific, social/political, spiritual, technological. These have been discussed in terms of the concepts, skills, attitudes and knowledge which can be developed within and across subject areas.

How far children with moderate learning difficulties can learn within a normal curriculum depends on how far teachers can provide them with access to the normal curriculum. All one can say at present is that there is much publication, discussion and practical experiment. The National Association for Remedial Education, for example, has changed its journal's title to "Support for Learning" reflecting a change in the remedial teacher's role from withdrawal teaching or teaching slow learner classes to a different role in mixed ability classes - supporting pupils and teachers and collaborative teaching. The Association has made close contacts with subject teaching associations. Remedial teachers have become support teachers working collaboratively with specialist teachers in classrooms. There are some examples of innovative practice which is making it possible for pupils with a variety of special needs to benefit from teaching in groups of mixed ability at least in the first three years of secondary schools. Some of the practical issues can be illustrated by an example. One school prepared for the change by having a year of discussion of the policy which involved all departments. At the end of the year, the whole staff voted on the policy and accepted it. The system has a coordinator based in a resource room but support teaching for much of the time. There is a link teacher in each subject department who provides curriculum support and other teachers also provide some periods of support. There is a weekly visit by an educational psychologist and assistance as required from the LEA support service and social services. The system works effectively (Giles and Dunlop, 1986) and other schools in the same town are striving in the same direction.

Many other schools are developing their own patterns but there are obviously differences between schools in the extent of need for support teaching help and also different attitudes in departments and among staff about this method of working. However, it is a development which has the potential of providing educationally retarded pupils with a more normal educational experience, together with help in 'basic' educational and social skills.

In brief, after 30 years of developments in, and attempts to define, the special curriculum we have returned to the difficult task of trying to provide children who have moderate learning difficulties with a fuller experience of a common curriculum. It is not a watered down curriculum which implies limiting the range of topics; rather one which accepts that pupils understand concepts at different levels and acquire skills to different degrees.

POST-SCHOOL AND FURTHER EDUCATION

Preparing pupils for life after leaving school has always been a major concern of teachers - perhaps the one uncontroversial aspect of their education. In Birmingham, an After Care department was set up early in the century to visit ex-pupils. In the late 1950s, a Leavers' programme was developed at St. Francis School (with some influence from Dr. Gunzburg's work with adolescent subnormals in the adjacent MD hospital) - visits to work places, interviews, form filling, budgeting and money, travel, leisure and other aspects of social competence. Later some special schools started to provide work experience until it was stopped by the Factory Inspectorate. However, this has now become a feature of all schools' provision and of MSC schemes. There was *even in the late 1950s,* a residential school which appointed a teacher solely to maintain contact with former pupils and to provide further education at a number of centres in the county. Later, link courses enabled special school pupils to have part-time experience at FE colleges during their final year. The college contribution was sometimes unsuitable in level but, in the recent expansion of F.E. for special needs, expertise has developed. As one college principal acknowledged, what has developed in FE and through the work of the FEU owes much to the developments in special schools (Baillie, 1982).

Formerly, nearly all ESN leavers left school at 16 and the majority went into a job. Follow-up studies indicated a reasonable adjustment to work and life. Atkinson had followed up 45 leavers (average age 20) in 1957. Thirty were in work and earning an independent living; 12 had experienced some difficulties. He traced 44 of them thirty years later. Thirty seven were in work, 31 entirely self-supporting; 9 had kept the same job for 30 years; 16 for 20-30 years. Fourteen earned between £100-£150 a week; one got £500! Seventy per cent could read, 17% were semi-literate and there were 12% non-readers, (Atkinson 1984). This sort of outcome seems very unlikely in the present situation - though some pupils do get jobs following leavers' programmes and work experience. Most pupils go on to FE courses for students with special needs and to MSC schemes. We must feel concern for those who do not find a job. As the studies by Atkinson and others show, getting a job provides a continuation of learning and experience. For others there is little to occupy their time; staying in bed to mid-day is a common result. Dependence on the family may be prolonged. Unemployment and lack of alternative occupation is a problem which the retarded have in common with other young people with significant disabilities, an issue explored by Tizard and Anderson (1983) who prepared a thoughtful paper on Alternatives to Work. It is my impression that we have not got much further in solving the problem.

CONCLUSIONS

The pattern of provision for MLD pupils seems to be beginning to change. Already some special schools have been closed, partly as a result of falling rolls, partly in a reorganization to establish separate secondary special schools- which of course need to be large enough to support staffing for a secondary curriculum.

There are also signs of cooperation and liaison between ordinary and special schools - part-time exchange of some pupils; out-reach or support services from special schools. There appear to be a variety of organized arrangements for MLD pupils in ordinary schools - some authorities have proposals for special centres in ordinary schools and many are in the process of developing their support and advisory services. The advantages of these alternatives need to be considered; and particularly the practical issues in making them work effectively. Units/special classes in ordinary schools can be relatively segregated without some of the advantages of the special school, e.g. USA experience. I do feel somewhat optimistic about the development of support systems in secondary schools. Backed by senior management, accepted by the staff and coordinated by support teachers of quality and competence, a development is in process which could provide more effectively for the majority of low attainers. Whether it can do so for pupils with the most marked educational difficulties is a question that only further experience and development can answer.

One thing is clear: that moves towards integrated provision requires INSET on a large scale in order to ensure that teachers have skills and understanding for teaching the wide range of ability. The new arrangements for funding in- service training of teachers puts a major responsibility on LEAs and schools to develop forms of in-service training to meet their needs, some of which are indicated by the growth points and new developments referred to earlier. The role of institutions of higher education in supporting these developments by infusing ideas and by providing experienced teachers with the opportunities for further study and enquiry remains uncertain. During the thirty years under review, it could be claimed that the expansion of provision for the educationally subnormal was supported and enriched by the special education courses offered in higher education. Such courses were the lift-off point for many careers as headteachers, advisers, lecturers, researchers and HMIs. It is right and appropriate that the new funding arrangements should aim to spread funding for training more widely but it would be unfortunate, to put it mildly, if that process led to the contraction and, in some places, disappearance of centres of specialist study and expertise in the education of pupils with mild, moderate and severe learning difficulties. Unfortunately, that already looks likely, given the financial pressures on institutions of higher education.

REFERENCES

Ainscow, M. & Tweddle, D.A. (1979) *Preventing Classroom Failure*. Chichester: Wiley.

Atkinson, E. (1984) The adaptation of educationally subnormal school leavers thirty years on. *Special Education,* **11,** 17-24.

Baillie, J. (1982) New initiatives - New hopes, *Special Education,* **9**,3.

Brennan, W.K. (1974) *Shaping the Education of Slow Learners*. London: Routledge and Kegan Paul.

Clarke, A.M. & A.D.B. (1958) *Mental Deficiency - the changing outlook*. 1st edition, London: Methuen.

Cheshire Education Committee (1956) *The Education of Dull Children at the Primary Stage*. London : University of London Press.

D.E.S. (1970) *Diagnostic and Assessment Units*. London : HMSO.

D.E.S. (1971) *Slow Learners in Secondary Schools,* London : HMSO.

D.E.S. (1975) *A Language for Life* (Bullock Report), London : HMSO.

D.E.S. (1978) *Special Educational Needs* (Warnock Report), London : HMSO.

D.E.S. (1983) *Statistics of Education* (Schools) London : HMSO.

Descoeudres, A. (1927) *The Education of Mental Defective Children,* London : Harrap.

Duncan, J. (1942) *The Education of the Ordinary Child,* London: Nelson.

Fleeman, A.M.F. (1984) From special to secondary school. *Special Education,* **11,** 23-6.

Frostig, M. & Horne, D. (1967) *The Frostig Programme for the Development of Visual Perception*. Chicago : Follett.

Giles, A. & Dunlop, S. (1986) Changing direction at Tile Hill. *Special Education,* **9**,1.

Gunzburg, H.C. (1957) *The Social Rehabilitation of the Subnormal*. London : Bailliere, Tindall and Cox.

Hallmark, N. & Dessent, T. (1982) A special education service centre. *Special Education,* **9,** 6-8.

Kirk, S.A. & Johnson, O. (1951) *Educating the Retarded Child,* Boston: Houghton Mifflin.

Lowden, G. (1984) Integrating slow learners in Wales. *Special Education,* **11,** 4.

Marra, M.E. (1981) The incidence and nature of secondary handicaps among children in day ESN schools, *Remedial Education,* **16,**2.

Ministry of Education (1946) *Special Educational Treatment,* London : HMSO.

Ministry of Education (1961) Circular 11/61. *Special educational treatment for educationally subnormal pupils.*

Piaget, J. (1952) *The Child's Conception of Number*. London : Routledge and Kegan Paul.

Rutter, M., Whitmore, K. & Tizard, J. (1970) *Education, Health and Behaviour*, London: Methuen.

Swann, W. (1985) Is the integration of children with special needs happening? *Oxford Review of Education*, **11**, 1, 3-18.

Tansley, A.E. & Gulliford, R. (1960) *The Education of Slow Learning Children*. London : Routledge and Kegan Paul.

Tizard, J. & Anderson, E. (1983) The handicapped adolescent, alternatives to work for severely handicapped people. In A.D.B. Clarke and Tizard, B. (Eds.) *Child Development and Social Policy*. Leicester: British Psychological Society.

Warnock, H. M. (1978) *Special Educational Needs. Report of the Committee of Enquiry into the Education of Handicapped Children and Young People*. Cmnd. 7212, London: HMSO.

Welsh Office (1984) *Inspector's Report on Special Units for Pupils with Moderate Learning Difficulty in Gwent*. Cardiff: Welsh Office.

Williams, P. & Gruber, E. (1967) *Response to Special Schooling*. London : Longmans.

Wood, A.E. (1929) Report of the Mental Deficiency Committee. London : HMSO.

CHAPTER 7

Professional Constructions of the Concept of Moderate Learning Difficulties*

Tony Cline

Department of Psychology, University College London, UK

INTRODUCTION

There have been important developments in special education in recent years. New legislation has been introduced. Terminology, teaching methods and ideas about the organisation of provision have been evolving fast. How has all this affected the way professionals define moderate learning difficulties? In this chapter the aim is to examine the perceptions of individual professionals in everyday practice. Perception guides action: research towards the amelioration of a handicapping condition must include an appreciation of how it is perceived by those who work with it.

The protection of individual rights in special education is now based on compulsory procedures that are outlined in detail in legislation. It is possible to examine, for all children with special educational needs, an explicit formulation of their needs and the provision to be made for them. These "Statements" have a formal status, cover a common range of issues, and have been read and (at least implicitly) accepted by the child's parents. They are developed by gleaning the advice of professionals with very different perspectives on child development and educational needs. The assessment procedure has standard features that will have been common for all the children. Whilst the regulations are permissive on the content

***Acknowledgement** The author would like to acknowledge with gratitude the advice and assistance of educational psychologists in the area, and of the head teacher of the school which participated. The support of the Inner London Education Authority, which gave permission for this study to be carried out in one of their schools is also acknowledged.

of these Statements, there is likely to be a degree of common coverage across individuals. This report draws upon Statements in seeking to answer the questions - how do professionals in an urban area now construe the concept of 'moderate learning difficulties' and what do they have in mind when they recommend 'a modified curriculum'?

Perhaps the strategy of studying this formal documentation will avoid one of the problems associated with the most common methods of conducting research in this field. This is that, when a research worker carries out semi-structured interviews (Tomlinson, 1981) or questionnaire surveys (ILEA, 1984), responses may be biased by subjects' own constructions of the purpose of the research. There are, of course, disadvantages: with 'unobtrusive measures' of this kind the data are more likely to be incomplete or irregular in ways that make systematic analysis difficult. Even so, useful research contributions on educational subnormality have been made in the past on the basis of this methodology (Williams and Gruber, 1967). The study reported here represents an attempt to explore the value for this type of research of the new format of Statements prescribed under the Education Act 1981. The content and ordering of these will, of course, be influenced by the writers' objectives, which might include:

- making a case to the LEA for the allocation of special education resources;
- offering positive support to parents at a time when they may be anxious;
- persuading teachers who may be asked to work with the child that this will be possible and rewarding;
- offering suggestions to the staff of the receiving school about educational objectives and methods.

An examination of such papers may throw light not only on the constructs professionals employ in this field but also on the relative weight they give to these possible objectives. The regulations and procedures are novel, so that what is examined is the product of initial strategies adopted for meeting the new requirements. It is likely that practice will develop further with experience of the new framework, so there is a particular value in a study at this early stage.

THE STUDY

The Statements examined were all those available for children admitted over a period of eight months to a day special school for children with moderate learning difficulties in a deprived urban area. (Six children were admitted without statements on the 'provisional' placements recommended in D.E.S. Circular 1/83 and were excluded from the study). This is a well established school in a modern building with a good reputation locally. The papers examined comprised both the LEA's Statement on each child and the professional advice attached to it. The method of content analysis was not comprehensive. It focussed on key areas of concern in the education of children with moderate learning difficulties that had been identified in advance.

1. Educational history
2. Abilities and attainments
3. Language
4. Social skills and behaviour
5. Medical information
6. Family background
7. Summary of special educational needs
8. Proposed special provision

For each heading the summary reference in the LEA Statement was noted if there was one. This note was supplemented if a reference in any of the professional advice added a substantially new element that was not covered in the Statement. No note was taken of repeated references to the same point by more than one professional.

Table 1 shows some characteristics of the borough in which the school is situated. It should be noted that a small proportion of the pupils live in neighbouring boroughs with different population profiles.

TABLE 1

Relevant Characteristics of the Borough (1985)

	Primary pupils (%)	Secondary pupils (%)
Parents unemployed	32	25
From one-parent families	29	33
Eligible for free meals	54	53
From families of 4+ children	27	32
English not spoken at home	31	27
Ethnic background other than EWSI*	61	59

*ESWI: English, Scottish, Welsh or Irish

The sample includes 26 children aged 4 - 14. It is atypical in that girls predominate and the age profile is not significantly weighted towards the secondary stage (Table 2). The number of pupils from black and ethnic minoritybackgrounds (15) is consistent with the overall percentage in the school population as a whole. There is no value in reporting detailed within-sample analyses in a study with such small numbers. But it maybe helpful to note, as background to later comments, that Afro-Caribbean pupils appeared to be slightly under represented and South Asian to be slightly over represented compared to their numbers in the general school population in the area. All but one of the children had been born in the United Kingdom, as far as could be ascertained from the papers.

It is not possible to provide a detailed account of the social and family experiences of the children, because many of the professionals contributing to the statements focus their observations closely on what is seen as directly relevant to the educational task. The papers do not provide general information on social background.

For some children it is clear that family factors had played a significant part in generating or exacerbating their learning difficulties. Many had shown serious emotional and behavioural problems in previous settings, together with the learning difficulties that led to their being placed in this school. These issues will be the subject of a separate report. However, the fact that some degree of emotional, social or behavioural difficulty was mentioned in 21 of the 26 cases will need to be borne in mind when considering the professionals' recommendations about provision. They did not enjoy the luxury of being able to distinguish neatly between the various manifestations of the children's vulnerability - a luxury available only to the research worker with no direct responsibilities for the children. It is only possible to do justice to the challenge they face by not losing sight of that dimension whilst focusing attention elsewhere

THE ACCOUNTS GIVEN OF THE CHILDREN'S EDUCATIONAL EXPERIENCES

In the context of the Education Act 1981 and current public debate it was to be expected that one concern of those preparing the Statements would be to explain and justify a decision that a child was to be educated in a segregated special school rather than in provision based in a mainstream establishment. A small number of the Statements tackled this issue by defining future aims for the pupil partly in terms of links with mainstream provision or (in one case only) eventual full-time transfer to an ordinary school. It was notable that these references were generally imprecise in relation to both timing and the nature of the anticipated linked programme. The contributing professionals may have taken for granted the established links which this special school has locally with some primary and secondary schools and colleges. It was rare for there

TABLE 2

Characteristics of the Pupil Sample

Sex:	Boys	11
	Girls	15
Age on admission	4—7 years	10
	8—10 years	7
	11—14 years	9
Ethnic background	ESWI*	12
	Afro-Caribbean	2
	South Asian	8
	Other**	4
First language	English	15
	Punjabi	4
	Bengali***	3
	Turkish	2
	Maltese	1
	Gujerati	1
4+ children in family		9
One or more siblings at special school		6

*ESWI: English, Scottish, Welsh or Irish **includes 2 Turkish-Cypriot, 1 Maltese and 1 Turkish-Cypriot/English ***includes Sylhetti.

to be specific advice on individual needs in this respect in the papers. Yet observations on children's earlier educational experiences can be helpful in suggesting which strategies for integration are most likely to be fruitful in the future. Where this is attempted in the papers, it is usually through indicating an area of the curriculum in which the child has shown particular talent or particular interest.

There are virtually no references to the teaching methods and styles that have been found to be most effective. The reason seems likely to lie in the function of these Statements in justifying the move to a separate special school. If the justification does not lie in detailed plans for integration in the future, it must reside in a general failure of this provision in the past.

The implicit or explicit line of reasoning in the case of children attending primary and secondary schools appeared to be:

a) The child has made very limited progress in an ordinary school.

b) Extra help has been provided in that setting or in an area special class on a part-time basis. Progress has still been very limited, and the lag compared to age peers has increased.

c) In most cases (but not all) a further effort has been made to support the child in ordinary school through more intensive forms of special help.

d) In some cases a crisis has been precipitated by the child's emotional or behavioural reaction to continued failure or by an external circumstance such as the imminence of secondary school transfer. In other cases the steady increase in the gap between the child's attainments and those of others has reached an intolerable level without any specific precipitating factor.

e) Transfer to day special school is now seen as the most humane or supportive or efficient response to the child's predicament. The facilities and methods of the school are seen as particularly suited to the child's needs in a way that the present school cannot match.

Thus these Statements reflect the emphasis of the definition of special educational needs in the Education Act 1981. As we shall see, they do record in detail how the children's difficulties in learning differ from those of their age peers. But in addition they give attention to the second question the Act poses - is there reason to suppose that these difficulties prevent or hinder them from making use of educational facilities of a kind generally provided for children of their age in the area?

In a significant minority of six cases the special provision arranged previously was designed for pupils with emotional and behavioural difficulties - a day special school for one child, a part-time area special class for two, a secondary school sanctuary unit for one, and a primary school nurture group for two more. Most of the South Asian children had had some extra provision for English teaching, but mother tongue teaching was not mentioned in any of the papers. In one case the teaching of English in a withdrawal group was the only special provision mentioned. It was clear, however, that additional resources in the ordinary school had been deployed flexibly and intensively in many cases with attention to the specific needs of the child, e.g. dividing time between remedial teaching of basic academic skills and support teaching in subject specialist classrooms with other members of the class group.

THE ACCOUNTS GIVEN OF THEIR LEARNING DIFFICULTIES

Intelligence quotients were the key point of reference in defining the population of this type of special school for many years. From 1945 the formal definition in Ministry of Education Regulations allowed for other factors to be considered, and very many pupils in the schools had IQs above the supposed maximum of the appropriate range. Textbooks of the period stressed that "the demarcation lines between the various groups cannot be rigidly fixed at certain IQ levels" (Lovell, 1958). Nonetheless the concept of a fixed level of intelligence within a particular range was fundamental to the development of provision for the educationally subnormal (moderate). IQs were classified according to a fairly simple system, such as that shown in Figure 1.

IQ	
160 145 130	Superior
115 100 85	Normal range of intelligence
70	Dull
	Feeble-minded or high-grade defective
55 40	Imbecile
25 10	Idiot

Figure 1
IQ Classification in a 1958 Textbook

Many of these terms soon went out of use. In recent years the concept of a fixed IQ and the technology of measurement associated with it have received even more severe and damaging criticism.

What constructs are professionals now using to define the intellectual abilities and the general level of functioning of the children they recommend for special schools of this type?

On the evidence of this small-scale study the picture is one of uncertainty and change. Clinical or educational psychologists had used named, age-related intelligence or developmental scales in their assessment of 11 of the 26 children. The Wechsler Intelligence Scale for Children - Revised had been used eight times either in full or in part. Five other scales were quoted once each - Stanford-Binet, Merrill-Palmer, Griffiths, McCarthy, and Wechsler Preschool and Primary Scale. In eleven other cases it appeared from the text that a similar normative test had been given, but it was not named or described in detail in the advice attached to the Statement. IQ figures were stated in only two cases, and functioning was defined in terms of specific age levels in a further five. Generally psychologists were more cautious about the precise accuracy of their results, using broad categories to describe the children's developmental or intelligence levels, including comments on reliability, and noting possible sources of cultural or language bias. Whilst the reasons for caution in this field are well understood, one result was that it was difficult to be sure what was implied by a particular summary phrase. The certainties of a model of fixed categories of current intellectual functioning survives. The phrases listed in Table 1 were selected from papers examined during this study. It will be noted that they pose many difficulties of interpretation..

The test scores confirm the picture arising from the school reports of a boy of average potential but with poorly developed skills in particular areas.

In developing a summary analysis of the child's current functioning the psychologists did not rely solely on test evidence. As some of the selected quotations make clear, they were often careful to draw together evidence from a variety of sources. The written advice does not always make that explicit, and it has to be inferred from the way conclusions are put together. Teachers' observations had a particularly important role in this context, and there were a small number of cases where parents' comments were quoted for the same purpose.

Table 3 only covers general constructs. Many reports also offered a detailed analysis of sub-skills which showed that children had particular areas of more effective performance or more severe retardation. Sometimes this was stated simply in terms of a discrepancy between general verbal/language functioning and general nonverbal/performance functioning. More often it covered highly specific sub-skills related either to test performance or to progress in particular areas of the curriculum. However, a more detailed

TABLE 3
Constructs Used to Describe
Children's General Level of Functioning

Overall B's scores .... were consistent with those of a child who is generally slow to learn and who needs a considerable amount of carefully planned and structured adult help

Functioning was generally slow and at a low level.

Functioning in the limited ability range.
Performed consistently at a limited level.
Scores suggest that she is functioning at quite a limited level of intelligence.

Functioning within the borderline range.
Functioning at or below the borderline level.

On a wide range of tests and activities S's performance tended to confirm the school's view that she was very much below the average in terms of general abilty. A level of general intellectual functioning which is considerably below average.
Functioning at the below average level.

The test scores confirm the picture arising from the school reports of a boy of average potential but with poorly developed skills in particular areas.

---

discussion of the child's comprehension and use of language was a common feature found in half of the papers. In analysing the children's use of language the professionals seemed to find it easier to ignore the inherited system of categories of intellectual ability. Criterion-referenced accounts are more common (found in two-thirds of the cases), though age-norm expectations clearly remain influential and are cited too. Although eleven of the children had learnt another language before English, a comment on their reported competence in that language was included in only two cases. There appeared to be a shared model of how language use develops in the school setting for an English speaker. But the various professionals did not show in these papers a similar shared understanding of the educational implications of attending a school where the language medium is one's second language. Although the children's general learning difficulties might make this issue even more acute in its implications, it is not often highlighted.

Attainment in basic academic skills is described in some detail in most papers of all but the youngest children. The extent of the educational retardation they show is very serious. The selected quotations from a range of professionals in Table 4 relate to the achievement of literacy. In nine cases test results were given with a comment on the reading age level attained by the child. But a more common strategy was to outline in summary the reading skills within the child's competence with an implied hierarchical model of skill development. This was also the preferred strategy in the analysis of achievement in mathematics, which will not be covered in this report.

TABLE 4
Constructs Used to Describe Children's Achievement in Literacy

Reads at about the 7 - 8 year level with better mechanical reading than understanding. (13 years).
Cannot identify all letters confidently or repeat all the alphabet. Is very interested in books and at the initial stages of reading. Handwriting is legible, and she is happy copying passages without understanding. (10 years).
She has some sight vocabulary .. Likes to read and sees herself as a reader, but does not really have the concept of print.. Does not make use of phonic cues.. Does not read for meaning. (9 years).
He has a sight vocabulary of ten words.. Isn't reading as such but is excited that he can now recognize words in printed books. Cannot write his own name. (7 years).
He cannot read and can only just recognize and write his own name. (7 years).

Many reports also give attention to other areas of the curriculum but tend to offer less precise accounts with short general comments, as shown in Table 5. It is common for these papers to refer to individual strengths or interests in particular subjects and activities, but rare for them to include specific suggestions for building on these strengths and interests in the special school setting. This was one of several indicators that the fourth of the possible objectives in preparing Statements - that of offering suggestions to staff who might work with the child - was given relatively low priority. It appears that the professionals who wrote the Statements placed considerable trust in the expertise of staff in the receiving school and saw no need to offer detailed educational prescriptions in these papers.

The overall picture therefore is one of persistent and growing - but not quite universal - educational failure. Academic performance and learning difficulties are described with clarity and confidence. But the challenging task of summarizing children's current levels of intellectual functioning leads to some uncertainty, if not confusion, in the papers. This may be traced to a cautious view of the propriety of quoting intelligence and developmental scale results combined with a long-standing view of the MLD category that makes referring

TABLE 5

Constructs Used to Describe Children's Achievement in Other Areas of the Curriculum

---

She joins in PE but lacks coordination and concentration.. Her drawings are at an immature state of development. (9 years).

His physical coordination is poor. He tries hard in PE but achieves poor results.. Especially in PE you can see the eagerness coursing through him making him tremble. (7 years).

She is able to cope with activities such as art and craft, PE, swimming, games and drama. She enjoys these activities and is able to participate at her own level while joining in with other children. (8 years).

Her drawing skills are less retarded than others. (8 years).

She enjoys and is good at drawing, painting and dance. She enjoys PE and has interests in dance and music. (10 years).

He does not usually seek out answers to situations and problems himself, being very dependent on adult support to even begin looking at what needs to be thought about.. He shows marked difficulty in understanding new ideas. Even though he can learn a word formula to satisfy on a question and answer basis, he cannot use the idea in other situations or build on it to make new ideas.. His creative work is akin to that of a three or four year old. (11 years).

---

to such results almost inescapable. The problem lies in the muddled conceptualisation of what effectively remains a handicap category label.

THE RECOMMENDATIONS MADE FOR SPECIAL EDUCATIONAL PROVISION

John Fish has argued that, following the Education Act 1981, "the chief determinant of the special school's function should be the curriculum it offers. It is no longer appropriate to group children according to their disabilities, when to do so encompasses a very wide range of potential ability, achievement, learning difficulties and personal needs." He outlined three examples of curriculum variation. In one case the content is similar in range and level to that taught to the majority in ordinary schools, but it is modified in terms of special techniques required to teach it. In another the curriculum is modified in terms of objectives and pace. "Such a curriculum, for children who are slow to learn or who have moderate learning difficulties, should be realistic in terms of what can be accomplished in the time available but have relatively high expectations. It should be much less dependent on literacy skills for access to the normal range of study areas than the ordinary curriculum." Thirdly, there is a curriculum "which places major emphasis on the development of social skills and personal autonomy designed for children with severe learning difficulties and degrees of mental retardation". This is, of course, closely similar to the model of three levels of curriculum postulated in DES guidelines on the subject. Fish had been a senior member of HM Inspectorate. The formulation in his book is particularly helpful in its consistent emphasis on the need for common aims for all children (Fish, 1985). It is the second variant, known as "a modified curriculum", that is particularly relevant to this study.

Twenty-two of the 26 statements include the phrase "modified curriculum" in the summary of the provision required for the child. It tends to be used as a form of shorthand without elaboration. In the few cases where a fuller explanation is given there are echoes of the points made above:

A modified curriculum appropriate to a slow learning child.
A modified curriculum which is geared to her pace of learning.
A modified curriculum suitable for children who have moderate learning difficulties.

In general the analyses focus on the implications of the children's particular difficulties in learning and adjustment. They do not draw attention to areas of strength on which an educational programme can build, but highlight aspects of special provision that will be required to make an adequate response to their problems.

Eighteen statements make an explicit reference to curriculum coverage. In the case of one twelve year old a recommendation is made for "a curriculum offering the widest possible subject based programme". In seven other cases it is stressed that the child needs special help across the whole curriculum. The phrase "a total remedial programme" is used in this connection. More often a particular emphasis on skills coverage is indicated relating it to the child's observed areas of weakness - basic literacy and numeracy skills (5), effective learning strategies (2), memory skills (2), self-help skills (2), language development (6), the use of English as a second language (1), and for a late entrant "an emphasis on the development of skills that are essential for when she leaves school".

For most professionals what was to be taught was only one issue; as much attention was given to how it was to be taught. They proposed that the learning programme should be more 'structured' or 'systematic'; it should emphasize active learning, counter a tendency to passivity and non-involvement, encourage independence and a greater degree of autonomy (5); it should offer consistent and clear expectations (1). The advantage for a particular child of a teaching group that is relatively homogeneous in ability is stressed in two cases. More often reference is made to other features of the special school - a small institution with fewer adults and children (7), small teaching groups (11), individual attention (7), and a 'supportive' atmosphere (7). The value of particular features for individual children is spelt out in detail in a third of the cases where they are mentioned: different advantages are sought for those with varying patterns of need. Usually these features are seen as a necessary context for particular teaching methods or management programmes. Frequently the emphasis is on developing confidence, self- esteem and social skills, and improving social adjustment rather than on educational objectives that are more narrowly conceived in 'academic' terms. There is a stress on creating the conditions for cooperative learning and relaxed communication. The special school setting is seen as a more favourable environment for a child who has become shy, anxious and withdrawn to develop more effective ways of relating to peers. Similarly it is seen as being able to offer containment ('clearly stated boundaries') to a boisterous and sometimes aggressive child who presents problems of management in the ordinary school.

The support of particular professionals who visit the special school regularly is seen as important in a minority of cases - medical oversight (3) and speech therapy (6). Child guidance support is also mentioned in two cases where clinics are already involved. Many of the children are reported by their parents to be difficult to manage at home, and the school is asked to support parents over this in seven cases. As would be expected, the children had experienced a variety of medical and social problems. They are not detailed in this report, but they do constitute a significant feature of theprofessionals' view of the children's needs.

CONCLUSIONS

This preliminary study in one school indicates that formal Statements prepared under section 5 of the Education Act 1981 are a useful source of evidence in the investigation of professionals' constructions of special education. They must be viewed in the light of the purpose for which they were prepared. In this sample internal evidence suggests that the primary objective in drafting Statements was to make a case to the LEA for allocating special education resources. There were indications that other possible objectives received less priority.

The concept of moderate learning difficulties encompasses great diversity, (see also chapter 3 by Richardson in this volume). Its historical roots lie in the notion of fixed levels of general intelligence, and the introduction of new terms has not resolved uncertainties that now surround that notion. There is no doubt about the serious nature and broad scope of the educational difficulties faced by the children admitted to this school. That picture emerges clearly from the reports examined in the study. At the same time the key terms used to summarize their educational needs are often ambiguous or unclear. There is evidence that the working model employed for moderate learning difficulties in the Statements is a version of the original model of educational subnormality that has been only partially reconstructed. Perhaps that is predictable when the school itself is an establishment with strong traditions that were developed when it had the earlier title. Its place and function in the overall pattern of LEA educational provision are virtually unchanged. If the influence of such factors is to be fully understood, it will be necessary to examine a larger sample of Statements from a variety of local education authorities. How far do professional constructions of moderate learning difficulties vary with features of the setting to which they relate? The findings reported above raise that question as well as the more fundamental one of what basis exists for a contemporary theoretical model of moderate learning difficulties.

REFERENCES

Fish, J. (1985) *Special Education: The Way Ahead.* Milton Keynes: Open University Press.

ILEA (1984) *Characteristics of pupils in special schools and units.* London: Inner London Education Authority.

Lovell, K. (1958) *Educational Psychology and Children.* London: University of London Press.

Tomlinson, S. (1981) *Educational Subnormality: A study in decision-making.* London: Routledge and Kegan Paul.

Williams, P. & Gruber, E. (1967) *Response to Special Schooling.* London: Longmans.

CHAPTER 8

Comparing Schools for Pupils With Moderate Learning Difficulties

Peter Evans, Patrick Redmond and Judy Ireson

Department of Child Development and Educational Psychology, Institute of Education, University of London

INTRODUCTION

The biggest single group of children with special educational needs are those that are now described as having moderate learning difficulties (MLD). Of this group of children a large proportion of those with more intractable problems find themselves being educated in MLD schools. In fact at our last count there were some 550 such schools in England and Wales. But what are these actually like? What do they do? How do they do it? Are there common aims and objectives? To what extent are the pupils making adequate progress?

Although questions of this nature have been addressed by authors such as Brennan (1979) no-one as far as we are aware has attempted to compare and contrast MLD schools as working organisations or to identify in any systematic fashion what the process of curriculum development is or how it takes place. In this chapter we wish to describe a first attempt at a comparative analysis of ten MLD schools which is based on a systematic data gathering procedure utilising in particular the framework for the evaluation of qualitative data based on the work of Miles and Huberman (1984). This sample includes West Oaks school which is described more fully in the next chapter.

THE SAMPLE OF SCHOOLS

The schools in the sample were selected by approaching LEA advisers and other knowledgeable individuals with the request that they should recommend schools that were providing a structured curriculum for their pupils. In addition we selected a school which had recently been the subject of an unfavourable HMI review.

Altogether there were ten schools from varying parts of the country. Yorkshire, North Wales, The Midlands, the South West of England, the South East of England and the London Area.

These schools were visited by either two or three members of the research team who conducted semi-structured interviews with the head and other key teachers. The questions that made up the interviews were derived from a model of school-based curriculum development that had been expounded by one of the research group. (Skilbeck, 1984) and which covered the areas of planning, development, implementation and evaluation of the curriculum. Interviews lasted for up to two hours and were conducted and maintained by one of the researchers while the other took notes. They were subsequently written up by the note-taker and confirmed by the interviewer. Other school documentation was also collected such as curriculum documents, and booklets for parents. Finally the information was validated by returning the typed reports to the respondents for their verification, and in two of the schools through additional visits. In addition a copy of the interview questions was included with each report and additional information was invited where it was felt that a question had not been fully answered.

We have given some attention to a full description of the method since it is clear that any subsequent comparisons rest entirely on the belief that we have been able to gather data equally fairly across the schools.

These data, it will be remembered, were gathered from a semi-structured interview that was planned around broadly based issues. However, because of the differentially prevailing circumstances in schools and LEA's this led to a very wide range of information being provided by the teachers. In order then to simplify the data to allow for comparisons between schools, categories were derived from the texts and the material was systematically allotted to these categories.

In exploratory work of this kind it is simply unrealistic to imagine that categories once created remain immutable. Particularly at the early stages it became necessary to sub- divide categories, change boundaries and names in order that they should accurately reflect the content of the information and its meaning. Initially this system was developed on a sample of reports and documentation. Eight of the MLD schools which had been visited by December 1985 were involved in this stage of the analysis. This led to a set of twenty categories which appeared to reflect aspects of the curriculum development strategies of the schools. In order to represent this process we have grouped these categories into an organised system. We like to think of this as a simplified representation of a complex organic system and it is made up of the twenty categories which were derived from the school data.

GENERAL FEATURES

The model that we have put together and which is shown in Figure 1 is intended to represent the process of curriculum development in MLD schools. Since it is intended to model a living system, all of the individual components must be seen to be interdependent. The model is nested with the implementation and pupil progress sections being at its core. This sub-process is seen as working in this way because teaching goes on in classrooms and will have degrees of independence from the remainder of the system. However, around it, the other elements of the system may be seen as operating at different levels in the system. So, for example, the sections marked as evaluation, curriculum decision making and intention may form one such level and external influences and parents another. Since any exact relationship between these features is at the present time unknown the model as represented in Figure 1 has a degree of uncertainty. The relationships between elements which we feel are more certain are indicated by continuous lines marked with arrowheads.

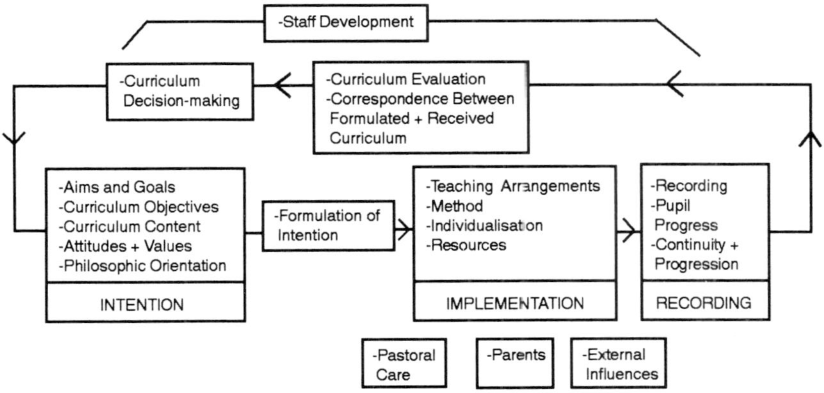

Figure 1
The interrelationship of categories in the curriculum development process.

SPECIFIC FEATURES

At the core of the model we have the two areas of IMPLEMENTATION and RECORDING. Under implementation there is *teaching arrangements* which refers to groupings of teachers and pupils for teaching purposes, *method* which describes teaching methods or instructional strategies used by teachers. *Individualisation* covers the use of individualised programmes of work including any specially designed schemes of work which are individually based and finally *resources* which includes reference to curriculum resources (which may or may not be available) which would be appropriate for classroom use.

In the conceptual area of RECORDING there are the categories of *recording* which includes records compiled to fulfil internal or external school requirements as well as teachers' own records; *pupil progress* which covers references to or indications of concern for pupil progress and *continuity and progression* which refers to the means by which the school ensures curriculum continuity for each child.

Moving on now to categories in the outer level which have less immediate influence on the classroom first there is EVALUATION. This comprises *evaluation* or the nature of the information that the school is using to make judgements about a part or the whole curriculum; *correspondence* which refers to the correspondence between the curriculum as formulated and as received. Next there is CURRICULUM DECISION MAKING which includes information concerned with the nature and extent of involvement of people in the decision making process that gives rise to the curriculum. The penultimate set of categories, of the part of the model linked by continuous lines is called INTENTION. This block consists of aims and goals or statements of *aims and goals* held by the school. *Objectives* includes any use of the term 'objectives' in behavioural or wider senses, curriculum content is any example of curriculum content in the form of subject areas or skills taught. *Attitudes and values* refers to interest displayed by the school or teachers in promoting positive attitudes and values as part of the stated or hidden curriculum and covers the underlying philosophy, principle or belief which helps to determine the overall school approach.

The cyclical nature of the model is indicated at this stage of the description by arrival at the INTENTION area, since clearly such descriptors could 'lead' the curriculum development process of the school. Indeed some schools may well have started out with the categories described here clearly in mind. Alternatively the ideas represented here may well have developed through the ongoing functioning of the school. However in both cases it is likely that the content of the categories would become elaborated and refined as the school progresses. The final category in the linked part of the model *formulation of intention,* may well reflect the outcomes of refinements referred to above, but formally it included statements of the curriculum intention in documentary or other form.

Three other categories were identified which at this stage we have not tied to the main flow of the model. *Pastoral care* covers statements concerning the well being and discipline of pupils; *parents* refers to statements covering the home background of pupils and parent involvement with the school. *External influences* includes issues relating to the external influences on the school and its curriculum.

Finally *staff development* includes the involvement of staff in workshops, in-service and other activities intended to develop their skills and practice within the school. This category is placed where it is since it became clear that the functioning of the whole process led to teachers being better informed about their practices in a way which may be thought of as staff development.

FURTHER ANALYSIS OF THE DATA

The data on all of the ten schools has been coded and categorised according to the system just described. Such a procedure permits a comparative analysis through the drawing up of a 10 X 20 matrix of schools by categories. This massive matrix was then examined with a view to detecting common patterns or trends across the schools for any of the categories which appeared to act as discriminating and/or common variables. Having done this the schools were arranged into three groupings of high, medium and low. These appellations referred to the degrees to which each school had attempted to structure its curriculum and it must be said that to a large extent the groupings resulted from an examination of data derived from school documentation stating the aims, goals and objectives of the curriculum. Where these were stated for all curriculum areas and were in evidence in the classroom the school was considered to be in the high level of structuring. If there was very little evidence of curriculum formulation or evidence that it applied to limited areas, such as individual subjects the school was considered to reflect a low level of structuring. A third group of schools emerged which occupied an intermediate position.

A full exposition of the data would require much more space than can be afforded here. However to illustrate the process it is worth considering one example of the category system as it emerged from the analysis in order to illustrate the method and some of the differences that appear to exist.

Table 1 shows the category of *'objectives'* and includes at the top the ground rule for placing statements into this slot. Next there are three sub-sections of high medium and low.

It may be seen that those schools that were placed high on our list (H1 - H5) all have objectives-based approaches to their curriculum which are in wide use in all curriculum areas.

For example school H1 had what it described as a closed curriculum analysed into sequences of behavioural objectives, and also onjectives written to generalise groups of objectives. In H2 individual, agreed, sequenced objectives exist in all curriculum areas, a

TABLE 1

Matrix showing information given for each of the ten schools for the category of 'objectives'. The matrix also gives the ground rule for allotting data to that category

OBJECTIVES	
Ground Rules: Include any use of the term 'objectives' in behavioural, or wider senses.	
High	
H1	Closed Curriculum analysed into sequences of behavioural objectives. All staff trained in Precision Teaching, training given to all staff who are left to decide when to use it. Objectives written to generalise groups or objectives
H2	Individual, agreed, sequenced objectives in all curriculum areas.
H3	In maths, the language and vocabulary are stated as behavioural objactives. Specific objectives (goals?) for major curriculum areas (eg To develop reading skills). School tried to tie in section of Ainscow + Tweddle programme to teach subskills but difficult to prepare a lot of material for every child. Used as required. The more finely structured one becomes, greater danger of isolating subskills from main skills.
H4	Objectives were agreed by staff and are listed for all curriculum areas.
H5	Objectives approach used with every child in the school.
Medium	
M1	Behavioural objectives only suitable for certain areas of the curriculum. School broke down curriculum areas into behavioural steps. Need for criteria for behavioural objectives which do not rely on percentage values.
M2	Exploit intellectual potential to full. Help pupils to gain satisfaction in an ability to produce creative/expressive work. Provide practice and expertise in social, survival and practical skills. Provide positive caring atmosphere wherein individuals can develop and grow. Objectives listed for independence training programme.
M3	To provide whole school curriculum, to ensure continuity of learning experience, to develop basic skills, to provide a programme of integrated studies or science as core, to provide opportunities for children to explore and develop aesthetic/ethical and spiritual aspects of the world etc.
Low	
L1	Teacher of leavers class thought that SNAP might be useful, though not necessarily with his particular group.
L2	Some use of SNAP in one curriculum area. Generally, staff found idea of teaching to objectives hard to come to terms with.

TABLE 2

Matrix of data for the three groups of special schools given by each of the major sections of the model shown in Figure 1

	High	Medium		Low
INTENTION	'Objectives' approach Concern for academic and social progress. Children as individuals. Major areas analysed into objectives.	'Objectives' approach Objectives In some areas.	'Primary orientation 'goals' as objectives Integrated approach.	Open/closed model. Aims recently agreed Some use of SNAP
FORMULATIONE OF INTENTION	xtensive documentation. Less well-formulated areas viewed as less successful.	Documentation mostly broad description/guidelines		Documentation in a few areas only
IMPLE-MENTATION	Fexibility of method. Resources developed by staff. High Degree of individualisation.	Resources classified to objectives Some indivualisation	Published schemes No reference to individual-isation	Published schemes Some worksheets developed by staff. Some individual programmes in isolated areas.
RECORDING	Records closely tied to curriculum, Systematic close monitoring Optimism. Continuity good, because of reviews.	Recent curriculum-based record. Reviews of children	Separate records. Continuity through informal liason.	Class teachers keep own records. Continuity through common schemes and teacher communication
EVALUATION AND DECISION-MAKING	Frequent evaluation based on records and reviews. Whole staff involvement led by headteacher. Far-reaching staff development. LEA/SPS highly supportive towards curriculum development.	Certain areas revised. Whole staff involved. Staff development difficult. No evidence of external influence on curriculum development.		Curriculum being revised. Problems in involving staff. Staff difficulties with objectives. Poor external support.
PASTORAL/ PARENTS	Positive pastoral approach Parents supportive, participant role.	Pastoral care via class teacher. Parents sceptical of special school.		Disciplinary problems. Parents visit re disciplinary matters.

| Vertical line to indicate differing positions within Medium group of schools.

general pattern repeated in H3, H4 and H5. Thus there was extensive development and use of objectives in these schools.

In the schools in the medium range objectives were agreed but to a lesser degree. For example in M1 behavioural objectives were only suitable for certain areas of the curriculum and in M3 they were discussed more in terms of intention rather than as they were actually used. Finally in the schools in the low range there were some inklings that objectives might be useful but in L2 staff found the idea of teaching to objectives hard to come to terms with.

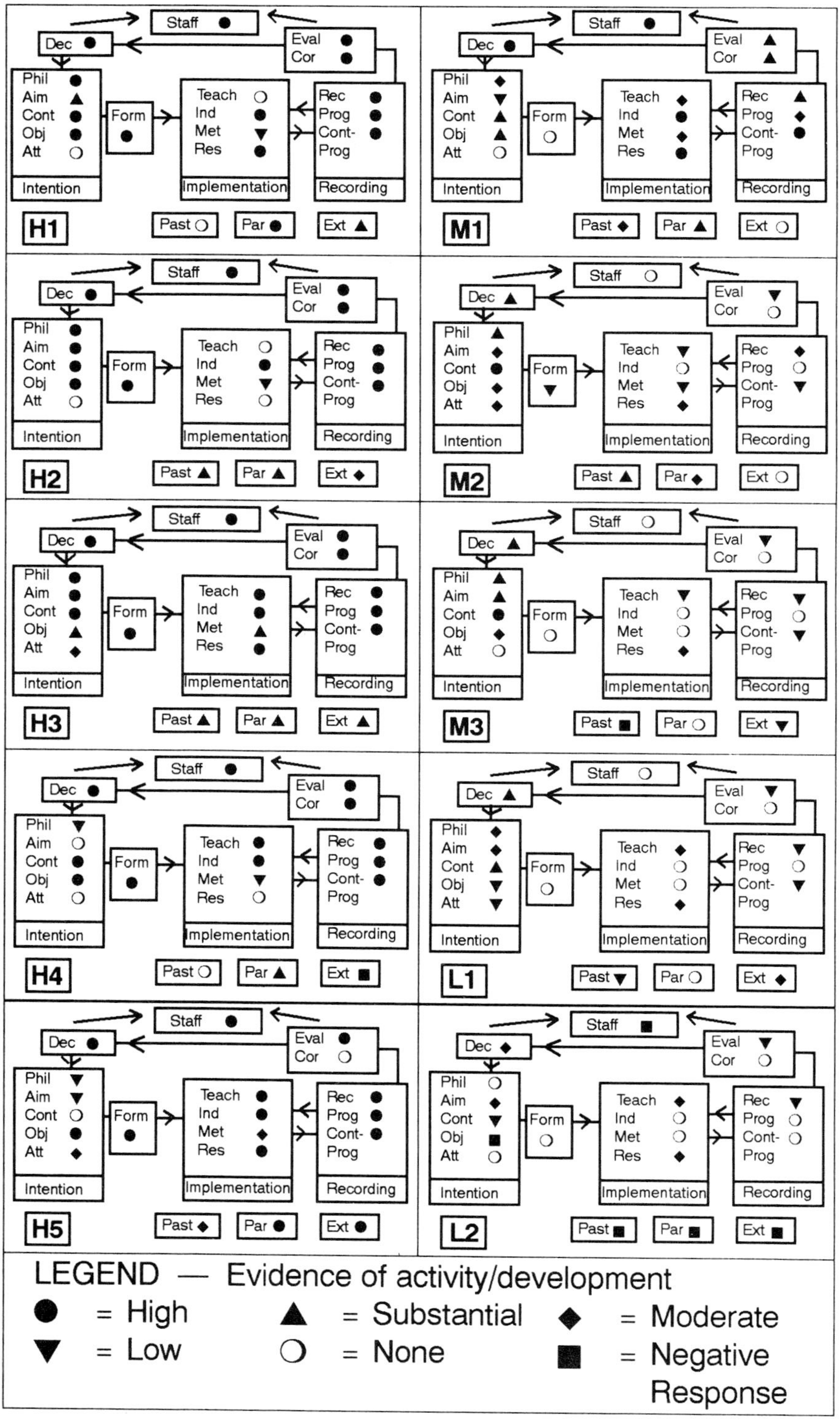
Staff
Dec
Eval
Cor
Phil
Aim
Cont
Obj
Att
Intention
Form
Teach
Ind
Met
Res
Implementation
Rec
Prog
Cont-
Prog
Recording
Past
Par
Ext
H1
M1
H2
M2
H3
M3
H4
L1
H5
L2
LEGEND — Evidence of activity/development
= High
= Substantial
= Moderate
= Low
= None
= Negative Response

The analysis that we have carried out is of course based on more than one category but a particular example has been chosen for illustration because of restrictions on space (for a full account see Evans et al 1987). However, we have attempted to provide a summary of all twenty categories and this is shown in Table 2.

Table 2 is a meta-matrix of the classification of schools into high, medium or low by the major areas of the curriculum development model as illustrated in Figure 1. For each of the areas eg INTENTION, FORMULATION OF INTENTION etc. through to PASTORAL/PARENTS it will be seen that the schools in the high, medium and low groups vary with regard to each of the areas. For example in the second one, FORMULATION OF INTENTION, the high group of schools shows extensive documentation with less well formulated areas being viewed as less successful. The medium schools describe documentation mostly as broad description/guidelines while the low group have documentation in a few areas only. The vertical lines in the medium schools are intended to show that for some of the areas there were differing positions in these schools that could not be collapsed sensibly into an overarching generalisation.

Once the reader has absorbed Table 2 it will be clear that these schools do differ quite considerably with regard to these main areas of the curriculum development model. Figure 2 shows these differences in a more pictorial form.

In Figure 2 we have attempted to represent the data from the tables exemplified in Table 1 as empty to filled circles according to the evidence of activity or development revealed. Whilst the exercise must be viewed in an impressionistic light it is immediately clear from the Figure that those schools on the left hand side, H1 to H5, do have a great deal more development in many of the areas of the model than those on the right hand side - with L2 showing some negative aspects. Perhaps some of the largest differences occur in the areas of classroom work ie implementation and recording where those schools in the medium and low range on the right hand side of the Figure particularly M2 and L2 show very little activity in these areas and categories in contrast to those H schools on the left hand side.

Figure 2 (opposite)

Impression charts showing levels of development within each category for each of the special schools (MLD). Category abbreviations: PHIL - Philosophic orientation, AIM - Aims and Goals, CONT - Curriculum Content, OBJ - Objectives, ATT - Attitudes and Values, FORM - Formulation of Intention, TEACH - Teaching Arrangements, IND - Individualisation, MET— Method, RES - Resources, REC - Recording, PROG - Pupil Progress, CONT-PROG - Continuity and Progression, EVAL - Evaluation, COR - Correspondence, DEC - Curriculum Decision-Making, EXT - External Influences, PAR - Parents, PAST -Pastoral Care, STAFF - Staff Development.

DISCUSSION

One of the worrying aspects of dealing with this kind of data is that the researcher always has the unnerving feeling that the apparent paucity of material especially in the 'L' type of school is leading to the differences that are being described. However, we feel that we have made every attempt to gather as full a set of data as possible in methodologically consistent ways and that the demonstrated differences reflect real distinctions between the schools. One of the important aspects that we believe the data reveal is the extent to which the process of delivering the curriculum can be made open to scrutiny. Without closer inspection of classroom practice and the teachers' own record books one just does not know if examples of successful teaching and record keeping are occurring in the majority of the M and L schools. It must be added that external follow up visits to two of them suggested that this was not happening in any systematic way and certainly not in a way that would serve to maintain continuity and to help develop the curriculum.

Three groups or a continuum? We have chosen to cluster these ten schools into three groups. We do not wish to argue that there is anything magical about this. To some extent it is a means to simplify the presentation of the data. Given more space it would be possible to discuss each of the ten schools separately and to treat the comparison as though they were on a continuum. We feel, however, that the data will probably not really stand this sort of fine treatment and because of this would probably add very little to the overall picture.

Tight and Loose Coupling. However, we do believe that we have been able to demonstrate fundamental differences between these groups of schools, particularly the H in contrast to the M and L combined, in the way that they function. This is perhaps best understood in terms of 'tight' and 'loose' coupling (Weick, 1985). The schools in the 'H' group have clearly developed to such a degree that the freedom of decision-making normally afforded to teachers has been supplanted by a collective mode of operating which is based on a rare and high degree of consensus over very specific details of curriculum intention. Each of the main areas of the model on p108 is not only *linked* (coupled) to the next but it also exerts a determining influence on what will happen in that area. Thus the high level of specificity which the 'H' schools have reached is bound to ensure that teachers follow the steps in a pre-determined sequence for each child. These sequences are assembled in such a fashion that they in turn generate their own means of recording progress thereby giving rise to an equally consistent and uniform approach to teachers own monitoring and recording procedures. Teachers thereafter are called upon to respond in the light of information gained via monitoring of progress thus creating a feedback loop into the overall curriculum framework which of itself shapes the teachers subsequent actions to help the child.

'Loose Coupling' on the other hand seems a more appropriate term to describe what is happening in the other groups ('M' and 'L' schools). The 'loose-coupling' of the remaining schools reflects much more closely the normal practice of schools in general. Within this kind of arrangement each of the component areas of the system (represented once again by the model) is much less directly influenced or determined by what is happening in other areas. Thus, the level of formulation of intention of the 'M' and 'L' schools has been taken only as far as is necessary to provide guidelines and general directions for further action. Both consensus and specificity are at a lower level, leaving teachers the freedom to develop further specificity if they choose, but not requiring them to do so. Since greater or lesser specificity combined with additional freedom of choice over individualisation, method and resources have implications for variable monitoring procedures, teachers are therefore free to record progress as and when they choose. Some indeed may follow a course similar to that of the 'H' teachers but, significantly, the system does not require them to do so. As for the setting up of a feedback loop in response to lack of success - that too is left to the discretion of individual teachers.

This description of the operation of the model within the 'M' and 'L' schools should therefore make it clear why the phrase 'loose coupling' is a particularly apt one. The curriculum development model allows for the presence of activity within each of its major areas simultaneously without the others being automatically affected by that activity. Clearly there will be some passing on of the effects from one area to another, otherwise the whole notion of attempting to implement an agreed curriculum is meaningless. But the variability of this 'passing on' of effect is a result of the loosely coupled relationships characteristic of organisations in general and schools in particular.

There are implied difficulties for some educationists in the notion of 'tight-coupling'. Much has been made of teachers' autonomy and professionalism in recent years. The assumptions behind such valued aspects of teaching rest on several premises, among which are such ideas as teaching as an art, flexibility and sensitivity to children's learning and freedom to respond in the light of the child's interest etc. 'Tight coupling' would be viewed by those who hold such positions as a severe restriction of teacher autonomy.

There are many other points that one could make but space does not permit. What we think we have shown is that it is possible to make systematic comparisons between schools that are meaningful and useful and may ultimately help to throw some light on what makes a good school and how it may be developed. In the second phase of our research we are working in a limited way on this issue.

CONCLUSIONS

This book is about the prevention and amelioration of mental handicap and it is clearly true that schools have a big part to play in this area of endeavour. It is also true to say that it is widely held that schools do make a difference and that some schools are more effective than others. These conclusions have generally been reached from research carried out in mainstream schools but the question is worth considering, in the light of the research reported here, albeit in the total absence of any comparative pupil outcome data.

If special education for mentally handicapped pupils is to mean anything then it must serve to ameliorate the problems that such children present in terms of organising their cognitions, emotions, social skills and so on. This is essentially a decision-making exercise in which schools must choose what and how to teach children which will be of most benefit. For such an endeavour to be maximally effective it clearly requires these decisions to be made on the basis of good data about pupil progress and how the rate of pupil progress can be improved. In addition the relevance of what these pupils are learning must also be justified.

We would wish to argue from the data presented here that this requirement of amelioration can be served best by the schools in the H group in contrast to those in the L. This is because the H group of schools have the necessarily fine level of data on which to base their decisions. For this same reason the additional feature of such schools would be that they are in a position to fulfil a requirement of secondary prevention. Through close monitoring and close coupling they are at least in a position to know how well their pupils are progressing and may make the necessary adjustment to meet their pupils' needs as they are seen to arise. Because of the forward looking way that such schools develop they are, in contrast to the L schools, in a position to tune their system accordingly.

While it would be interesting at some point in the future to compare these different forms of school organisation with regard to pupil outcomes, such an exercise would be bedevilled with difficulties, given the individual nature of the special needs of the children found in MLD schools and differing criteria of what would best reflect some generalisable notion of best outcome. In the meantime we believe that developing an understanding of schools as systems and how they can best develop to meet the individual pupils' needs, that surely they must, is a more appropriate and attainable goal.

In the next chapter one of the H schools is described in more detail.

REFERENCES

Brennan, W.K. (1979) *Curricular Needs of Slow Learners,* London: Evans/Methuen Educational.

Evans,P., Redmond, P., Ireson, J., & Wedell, K. (1987) *Curriculum Research for Pupils with Moderate Learning Difficulties.* DES project report No. MLD 87 (2). London: Department of Education and Science.

Miles, M.B., & Huberman, A.M. (1984) *Qualitative Data Analysis: A sourcebook of New Methods.* London: Sage.

Skilbeck, M. (1984) *School-Based Curriculum Development.* London: Harper and Row.

Weick, K.E. (1985) Sources of order in under-organized systems: themes in recent organizational theory. In Y.S. Lincoln (Ed.) *Organizational Theory and Inquiry: The Paradigm Revolution.* London: Sage.

CHAPTER 9

The Role of a Special School in the Amelioration of Mental Handicap

Mike Robertshaw

Leeds City Council, Advisor in Special Needs, Department of Education, Leeds, UK

INTRODUCTION

The previous chapter in this book by Evans, Redmond and Ireson provided a comparative description of the functioning of a set of special schools for pupils with moderate learning difficulties (MLD). One of the schools, H2 in Table 1, page 106 is the school which is to be the focus of the present chapter. This, then, is presented in the form of a number of case studies of individual pupils with the intention not only of providing a detailed account of the working of a school based on a skills analysis model (e.g. Gardner et al, 1983) but also to flesh out the skeleton description given by Evans, Redmond and Ireson.

West Oaks School is a local authority maintained special school in Leeds designed to meet the needs of children with profound, severe and moderate learning difficulties. It is a purpose built school and was opened in September 1976 with myself as headteacher and a staff specifically chosen to work with children with a wide variety of learning difficulties. There are approximately 125 children on roll, ranging in age from two to nineteen years and in ability from children with profound and complex learning difficulties to those with moderate learning difficulties. There are seventeen teachers, nine non-teaching staff, a nurse and the usual visiting medical and paramedical services.

The school has an approach to children based on their individual needs. This seeks to determine precisely what the children's needs are, to try to meet them through the construction and implementation of individual teaching programmes and to use the evaluation of their success as a guide for designing future learning programmes. Their content is derived directly from the school's skills-based curriculum and is one in which teaching is directed towards adding a variety of new skills to each child's repertoire of behaviours. These are organised into groups and hierarchies so that the child learns specific skills that then form the basis for other higher order skills. With careful organisation a child's learning can be structured to ensure that teaching is aimed at a particular skill development so that the teacher can, on the basis of knowledge of the child, decide what to teach at any stage of that development.

All learning can be viewed in this way, as the acquisition of a component of a skill, of a complete skill or of a group of skills. Some are easily dissected into discrete tasks for teaching purposes, others, for instance those involved in creative thinking or problem solving, can be more difficult to dissect. The working out of skill hierarchies enables the teacher to map out a plan for teaching. Clearly defined targets ensure that the teacher knows when teaching is successful, that is, when the child performs the skill to a specific level of competence. Lower order skills form the basis for the learning of higher order skills.

CASE CONFERENCES

The forum for deciding what a child needs to learn is the case-conference. These are held for every child in the school every six months. They are chaired by the headteacher and involve all adults working with each child. The child's class teacher is responsible for the preparation of material for each case. This consists of an assessment of the success of the previous case conference objectives and a proposed set of new objectives for a further six-month period. These targets are discussed at length and decisions are made about the next series of objectives based on criteria such as the age-appropriateness of the task, the practical use of the skills to be taught, the effectiveness of various teaching techniques and the comprehensive nature of the child's individual teaching programme. The objectives once identified are prioritised and listed under various headings with reference to the skills as listed in the school's curriculum. Individual teachers are then left to organise the teaching of the agreed objectives and this is usually done via the individual teaching programmes written for each child. This process will perhaps be best illustrated through the discussion of a number of case studies.

From a methodological viewpoint the data offered are derived, in the main, from single case study designs with changing criteria. They are based on information recorded as part of the child's on-going assessment process and not material designed to be used for empirical investigation.

Case study of John. John is a boy of sixteen. He has severe learning difficulties and a history of very violent behaviour towards adults whom he likes, in particular towards his immediate family and his class teachers. This behaviour has taken a great deal of time and energy to control, to the detriment of his education, but he is now much improved and it is necessary to attempt to provide him with as many skills as practicable to enable him to lead as full a life as possible in the future. At a case conference his previous history was discussed and new objectives were formulated on the assumption that he was to move towards some sheltered accommodation and some form of social education centre placement. The school's curriculum includes life and social skills as a core area. Table 1 indicates its main content.

TABLE 1

Life and Social Skills

Component Areas	**A. Domestic Skills**
Section 1	Clearing a table
Section 2	Setting a table for tea break/snack/breakfast/main meal
Section 3	Washing up
Section 4	Making the bed
Section 5	Room management
Section 6	Use of domestic equipment and tools
Section 7	Care of kitchen
Section 8	Preparation of drinks
Section 9	Preparing cold food
Section 10	Hot food preparation
Section 11	Use of kitchen equipment and tools
Section 13	Hygiene in the kitchen
Section 14	Handwashing clothes
Section 15	Machine washing clothes/ironing/simple repairs
	B. Movement in the Environment
Section 1	Movement within school
Section 2	Movement in the community
Section 3	Shopping
	C. Use of Amenities
Section 1	Telephone
Section 2	Vending machine
	D. Leisure
	Leisure time activities
	E. Social Relationships and Temperament

One item selected from section 9 of domestic skills is concerned with preparing cold food. A particular example "making a jam sandwich" may be used to illustrate further the working of the curriculum. It may appear that that this instance has been taken at random, but further examination of the list in Table 2 shows that this is not so and indicates that it is part of a planned series of other important skills.

TABLE 2

Curriculum Area: Life and Social Skills

	A. Domestic Skills Section 9. Preparing Cold Food	T	M	C	C2
9.1	Butters bread with supervision				
9.2	Butters bread unsupervised				
9.3	Makes a sandwich with supervision				
9.4	Makes a variety of sandwiches:- Jam, paste, egg, cheese — unsupervised				
9.5	Prepares fresh fruit, e.g. peels orange, unzips banana, washes apple				
etc					
9.14	Makes a variety of cold meals without supervision from fresh and/or prepared food				

The columns on the right marked T, M, C, C2 stand for "taught", "mastered", "checked" and "checked again" and are used to plot a child's progress. Inspection of the list of skills will reveal how the making of a jam sandwich fits into the overall pattern of the child's development.

Teacher's professional skill is used to individualise the teaching of each item to suit each particular pupil's needs and the teacher's individual teaching style. In many cases however, this is done by using an individual teaching programme as shown in Table 3.

This programme Table 3 clearly takes into account this student's individual needs and it would be different for a child with markedly different abilities and attitudes. Pupil progress is recorded in some detail by noting the date on which the skill was achieved and the prompts that were necessary to encourage task completion. It is in this way that the organisation of this particular school attempts to deal with the problems of learning caused by mental handicap.

TABLE 3

Life and Social Skills — Domestic A 9.2

Objective: Butters four slices of bread, spreading butter all over bread—not just in the middle of the slice.
(Note: after buttering bread he can then go on to make the jam sandwich)

Name: John

	Date skill achieved		
	25/2	1/3	14/3
1) Butters first slice to edges	*i*	*i*	▼
2) Butters second slice to edges	*i*	*i*	✓
3) Butters third slice to edges	*i*	✓	✓
4) Butters fourth slice to edges	*i*	▼	✓

Scoring:
✓ = no help
▼ = verbal prompt
9 - gestural prompt
p = physical prompt

Case study of Christopher. Christopher was admitted to the school shortly after its opening. He had been on a waiting list from a local primary school for a special school placement for a number of months and was referred mainly because of his bizarre behaviour. He is the eldest child from a small middle class family who suffered some early emotional deprivation due to his mother's prolonged postnatal depression. There are no specific known causes for his abnormality. At his primary school he had presented as a verbally precocious child with bizarre obsessive conversation, with high anxiety levels and difficulties in some areas of the curriculum.

He had become something of a joke with his peers which heightened his anxiety and led to his transfer into the special education sector, something, perhaps, that would not occur so readily in today's educational climate. However, the following figure allows one to trace his progress throughout his time at the school.

As may be seen from Figure 1 his abilities on entering school differed from subject to subject. His reading level as assessed by the Daniels and Diack test was interestingly higher than his chronological age though it must be said that this was recorded at an accuracy level and does not reflect levels of meaning or understanding - similarly, he had number skills which did not appear to be significantly delayed. The case discussions which took place at this early stage to some extent reflected this pattern and revolved around the concern that first he should maintain his age appropriate skills in literacy and numeracy. Secondly, that he should improve his performance levels in those areas in which he was failing, and thirdly

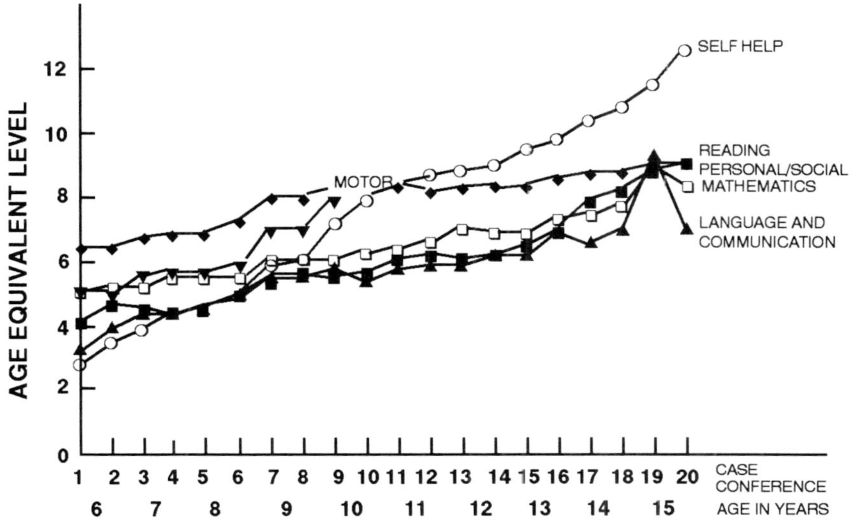

Figure 1
Figure showing the progress of Christopher in the curriculum areas of motor, self-help, reading, personal/social, mathematics and language and communication over nine years at the school.

and thirdly that he should seek to reduce his anxiety levels so that he could quickly return to the mainstream sector. His problem was basically seen as being of a psychiatric nature.

This early planning did in fact prove to be appropriate in terms of prioritising his learning, for as Figure 1 reveals, by case conference No. 4 he was continuing to make progress in the area of reading and language skills. His self-help skills had also significantly improved. This was brought about by requiring him to respond more appropriately to questions from adults and peers and also by strengthening his level of independence.

A look at the objectives set at this time confirms this development. (Table 4)

The objectives planning sessions then followed a fairly stable pattern with recommendations being made to pursue progress along all fronts until Christopher was approaching the age of ten when some significant changes were planned. It may be seen that at this stage (Case Conference No. 8) he had achieved personal and social skill levels of around the 5.5 year level, self-help skills of 6 years, language and communication skills of 5.3 years, number skills of 6 years, motor skills of 7 and reading skills of 8.00 years. Important decisions were being made at this time to shift the emphasis of approach. The initial plan, it will be recalled, was to attempt to try and accelerate the rate of learning in the areas of reading and number and to improve conversation skills in order to facilitate a return to mainstream schooling. At this stage in his school

TABLE 4

Objectives for Christopher, April 1977 Age 6

Reading

Christopher will:-	(a)	complete Pirate Book 4
	(b)	answer simple questions about stories read
	(c)	put sentences about stories into sequence

Language and Communication

Christopher will:-	(a)	put pictures in sequence to make story
	(b)	relate story displayed in pictures to teacher
	(c)	use complete sentences to express needs to teacher and other children

Number

Christopher will:-	(a)	add to 10 with counters
	(b)	tell time to hours
	(c)	say value of coins to 20p
	(d)	recite days of the week in order

Self Help

Christopher will:-	(a)	put on own coat
	(b)	put on own socks and shoes
	(c)	organise his own work materials on request
	(d)	put away apparatus and equipment appropriately

Personal/Social

Christopher will:-	(a)	greet adults appropriately
	(b)	run simple errands to school office
	(c)	play with 'named child' for up to five minutes
	(d)	share group equipment without becoming anxious

Motor

Christopher will:-	(a)	block colour simple shapes
	(b)	thread small beads
	(c)	jump over rope 6" from ground
	(d)	forward roll
	(e)	walk along beam unaided

life, however, it was becoming clear that Christopher's problems were developing in a different way from the direction envisaged and thus it was decided that a change of emphasis would be in his best interests. His reading ability, although improving was, it seemed, failing to accelerate in spite of specialised intensive teaching, particularly in relation to comprehension levels. As a consequence the school needed to consider closely what the future might hold in store for this child and whether the correct steps were being taken to meet his likely future needs. It will be clear that his social and self-help skills were at a much lower level than others. His operational level, in reality, was that of a five to six year old. This was caused, it seemed, by an overprotective family life and an inhibition to extending his level of personal skills brought on by anxiety. It was therefore decided that self-help and social development should attain a higher priority in order to raise his level of functional competence. Figure 1 reveals the extent of this re-allocation of teaching emphasis by the way the rate of attainment in this area improved. In other words, to spend hours of teacher time on reading and number skills was not proving to be an efficient use of time in relation to the rate of improvement when taken in the context of Christopher's perceived future needs.

A second significant change came at case conference 15 when Christopher was thirteen. It is at this stage in a child's development that a school ought to look to the future and attempt to predict what the long term prospects of a child might be. In Christopher's case, because of a combination of factors, it seemed unlikely that he would be heading for open employment, thus sheltered employment seemed to be the more likely eventual outcome. It also seemed probable that Christopher would require a form of sheltered accommodation at some time and so, once again, decisions were made about the nature of the programmes offered to him. It seemed clear that the self-help area which had shown real signs of development should be pursued and developed since it is these skills that make children and adults functionally competent in the world. The results of this decision are again reflected in the mount of progress recorded in the curriculum area of self-help skills.

A further significant time in terms of decision making is approaching again soon when preparations for leaving school at some age up to nineteen years are made. These decisions will determine what steps are to be taken to prepare him for the next stage in his life. They will inevitably involve out of school activities leading to independence training. To demonstrate this development Table 5 shows the current list of objectives for Christopher.

TABLE 5

Objectives for Christopher, December 1986 Age 15

Number		
Christopher will:-	(a)	handle combinations of coins to the value of £5 on request
	(b)	record addition of cost of 2/3 items to the total value of up to £5
	(c)	record change from £1
	(d)	tell time to five minutes
	(e)	estimate the cost of ten common household items
Language		
Christopher will:-	(a)	read for pleasure books from local library
	(b)	change own library book, choosing something appropriate NB. Does not pick first one he sees
	(c)	extend spelling vocabulary through personal diary at the rate of one word per day
	(d)	keep a diary of personal experiences
	(e)	write and illustrate books on topics of own choice
	(f)	tell group how to carry out a simple task
	(g)	make own shopping list
Personal/Social/Self Help		
Christopher will:-	(a)	cross main road in village with minimum supervision
	(b)	shop, accompanied by another student for up to five items in three shops using own list
	(c)	find six items in supermarket. Hand appropriate money at checkout and pack shopping
	(d)	prepare a simple snack involving the use of tin opener and electric hob
	(e)	follow a simple recipe including weighing to 2oz unsupervised
	(f)	shave using disposable razor
	(g)	wash and iron a simple garment
	(h)	set table for four persons, make tea and toast for all, clear away and wash up.

Readers might like to compare these objectives with those given in Table 4 when Christopher was much younger.

It will be recognised that a school has an important part to play in providing relevant educational experiences and that by constantly re-appraising its teaching programmes and prioritising learning experiences it can, to some extent, over a period of time, attempt to compensate for a developing condition such as the one described.

There are of course additional factors involved. When a child is at a school for ten years or more a change in emphasis can often act as a motivating factor resulting in accelerated performance in some areas. The dramatic changes described do not occur so abruptly in the school's thinking as may be implied here and doubts about the appropriateness of education are raised often before major changes are implemented. The school involvement in an individual problem of a very different kind is illustrated by considering the case of Susan.

Case study of Susan. Susan is of Afro-Caribbean origin. At the time of the following incident in her life she was fifteen years old, stood six feet tall, weighed nearly eleven stones and took size ten shoes. She was, and I suppose still is, a big girl!

Susan was admitted to the school because she had been suspended from her previous schools for persistent violence. West Oaks School has some interest, experience and expertise in dealing with children with behaviour problems and it was expedient to place her in a local assessment centre for an examination before taking her into the school. Her home background was materially good. Before being admitted to the assessment centre she lived at home with her mother and one older sister. Her other brothers and sisters had already left to set up homes of their own and follow various professional careers.

Susan functioned below her age level in all areas of the curriculum with a few tiny peaks of ability. She was, for example, an obsessively neat handwriter and had odd mathematical skills being able, for example to tell anyone on which day of the week they were born if she were given their date of birth. It was her behaviour however which had given most cause for concern in the past and which had singled her out as being handicapped in the eyes of the community.

Susan became violent if she did not get her own way. The violence was then used as a lever to secure her desires, a lever used extensively and effectively at home where her mother became a slave to it as she became physically unable to dominate her. At her various schools she had, in the past, used aggression to others as a means of dictating events and obtaining adult attention. This violence generally took the form of premeditated attacks on children smaller than herself (ie everybody!) and was executed almost always without a show of anger or excess physical activity but coolly and often with a smile for those adults to whom the violence was directed. Once she had obtained adult attention by way, usually, of vehemently expressed disapproval of her actions she would take steps to prolong it by asking questions repeatedly such as 'Why have I been naughty miss?' and 'Tell me again miss what I did wrong?'.

For the first four weeks that Susan was in school there were no violent incidents. She made friends and appeared to be happy. Then, after the honeymoon period was over the violence appeared. The first strategy, since the behaviour was apparently an attention seeking device, was as far as possible, to ignore the behaviour. This was not an easy plan to adopt as the safety of others was involved. However, we did try to limit the amount of attention she received after each incident. The pattern of events then gradually developed as follows: On the Monday of week five (marked as 1 in Figure 2) she pushed over a small child in the presence of a member of staff. She showed no remorse and seemed to want to pursue the admonition she received. On Wednesday, Thursday and Friday of the same week there were similar incidents. A new strategy was therefore decided upon to attempt to make her attacks on children non-rewarding.

The method decided upon was to isolate her in a small windowless room with a member of staff each time she attempted a violent act. There was nothing in the room but two chairs. The teachers were instructed to have no conversation with her about anything and to take the role of a guard. The thinking behind this was that if it was attention that she wanted as a result of her actions then we would

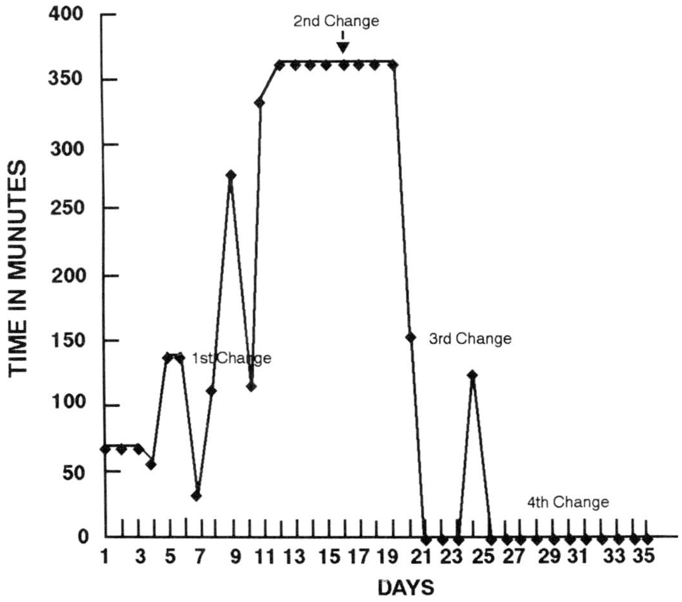

Figure 2
Figure showing changes in the amount of time Susan spent in isolation over time during the course of her first seven weeks in the school.

provide completely the opposite. If the incidents occurred during lesson time Susan was removed for the rest of the lesson. If they took place in free time then she was isolated for the rest of the free time and the whole of the next session. Careful records were kept of this course of action and the pattern of events over a six week period was as shown as follows:

Day	**Session (4 per day)**	**Time in minutes**
Monday(1)	Break am session 2	70
Tuesday(2)	Break am session 2	70
Wednesday(3)	Lunchtime session 3	70
Thursday(4)	Break pm session 4	60
Friday(5)	Session 1	} 135
Friday	Break am session 2	

On Friday Susan made the claim that "she was going to get moved from the school like she had been removed from all the others she had attended". By this we presumed she meant that she would behave so badly that we would exclude her. The battle was on!

Susan began this week with an immediate challenge in order presumably to back up her threat. The pattern of events was as follows:-

Day	**Session (4 per day)**	**Time in minutes**
Monday (6)	Session 1 & session 2	135

At this point it was decided to isolate her for the remainder of the day after the incident took place. This was to strengthen our response and to avoid incidents which might continue to reward her.

	Session (4 per day)	**Time in minutes**
Tuesday (7)	Break pm	45
Wednesday(8)	Session 3	120
Thursday (9)	Session 2	270
Friday (10)	Lunch time	150
Monday (11)	Session 1	330
Tuesday (12)	All day	360
Wednesday (13)	All day	360

It was necessary to collect Susan straight from her taxi:-

Day	**Session**	**Time in minutes**
Thursday (14)	Collected from taxi	360
Friday (15)	Collected from taxi	360

By now we were in a situation where Susan was being isolated all day and looked after by a team of teachers in half-hour shifts with still no conversation or interaction with her despite her attempts to escape and her occasional physical and verbal attacks.

Day	**Session**	**Time in minutes**
Monday (16)	Collected from taxi	360
Tuesday (17)	All day	360
Wednesday (18)	All day	360
Thursday (19)	All day	360

On Thursday Susan refused to get in the taxi to come to school. It was decided that we should go and fetch her to eliminate this strategy as a means of escaping the consequence of her behaviour.

Friday (20)	Session 1 and 2	150

Friday lunch-time was a highly significant turning point in the programme. Susan displayed a marked change of attitude after perhaps the worst morning we had ever had with her. She claimed that she wanted to go back to her classroom and did not want to be treated as she was. Such was the apparent change that we allowed her to return to her normal timetable that very afternoon.

It was decided at this point to allow Susan full access to the curriculum on a trial basis and further to tinker with the curriculum to allow her more access to the things that we knew she liked in order to make clear to her the difference in her life if she behaved as we wanted her to. She was thus allowed more time in needlework and home economics and members of staff were encouraged to give her their attention just so long as she was behaving appropriately.

Day	**Session (4 per day)**	**Time in minutes**
Monday (21)	-	-
Tuesday (22)	-	-
Wednesday (23)	-	-
Thursday (24)	Session 3 (weak and provoked)	120
Friday (25)		

At this stage Susan was returned to her normal timetable. Apart from occasional lapses which could be controlled with a verbal signal, she enjoyed a life in school without further major incident for about ten months when, because of home difficulties, she was removed to a different area.

This particular case has been outlined for a number of reasons. To begin with it demonstrates how a school as an institution can, if it has the will and the expertise, plan strategies which can lead to changes in difficult behaviours in children which have remained unchanged in other settings. It can do this because of the expertise and commitment of its staff and because there are in a school a comparatively large number of people who can share the work for a relatively short time each day. It is obviously more difficult for untrained staff and understaffed establishments to do the same. Although the school in taking on the problem was successful in controlling Susan's behaviour we did, in reality little service to those whose responsibility was to care for her outside of school hours which was, in fact, the largest proportion of the day. Her mother was physically unable to prevent her leaving the house and the resulting incidents involving the police eventually led to her being removed into care. Behaviour problems subsequently occurred in residential settings and her management was never generalised to those settings despite efforts to pass on management strategies. This is not to imply criticism of those establishments it merely emphasises the difficulty in maintaining a consistent regime in a number of different settings where staffing levels, training requirements and operating conditions are different. This lack of generalisation is often used as a criticism of a behavioural approach and it could be argued that an approach which sought to deal with the possible reasons for the behaviour would be more effective in the long term in cases of this kind. To some extent the approach adopted and strategies used in this instance were forced upon the school by the situation. We could have kept on asking Susan why she acted as she did but we might have had some difficulty getting rid of the bodies! The school did, in fact, demonstrate that using a planned approach it could significantly change the behaviour of a child and in Susan's case it helped to keep her out of residential care of a punitive nature until she left the school. It was a sufficient control to maintain her link with the real world!

Susan, on leaving school, became a persistent offender with menacing behaviour and assault as her major crimes and unfortunately was ultimately imprisoned as a means of removing her from society.

This case raises more issues than there is space to deal with here. On the one hand it could be looked upon as a success story as far as the school is concerned and indeed the school did manage to achieve what others had failed to do. On the other hand the failure of the girl to generalise any of this control to other settings and her eventual fate could presumably point to failure. Whatever the interpretation of this somewhat extreme case it does demonstrate how a school can intervene in a child's life to change significantly behaviours which are unfortunate manifestations of a handicapping condition and which if removed can lead to greater acceptance in society. Indeed, West Oaks School has for a number of years intervened in such a way in many cases. The fourth and final case raises different issues.

Case study of Mary. Mary has athetoid cerebral palsy. She was illegitimate. Her mother has a long standing psychiatric problem which has caused her to be hospitalized at fairly frequent intervals. Mary has never lived at home. As a baby she was kept in hospital until a place was found for her at a Dr Barnado's children's home where she has lived ever since. Her mother retains contact with her in an inconsistent way but occasionally has the child home to stay with her. Mary remains in the care of the Local Authority.

The child was admitted to the school at the age of four and has had the benefits of continued care in the same children's home and the same school until the present time. This is an example of how a school deals with various other agencies in attempting to provide for the needs of children such as Mary. Many regular routine interventions have been omitted from this description because of space, for example, there is no mention here of regular annual medical examinations, the regular bi- annual meetings with Dr Barnardo's or the Social Services reviews of children in care.

First, in order to give some indication of her ability level it is useful to look briefly at the objectives which were set for her at her first case conference.It will be appreciated that Mary is a child with profound and complex learning difficulties.

Mary, Age 4 October 1977

Gross Motor

Mary will:-	(a)	sit unsupported for up to 5 minutes
	(b)	stand with the aid of a frame for up to 5 minutes

Fine Motor

Mary will:-	(a)	pick up objects placed in front of her on the floor, sitting-supported.

Hearing and Language

Mary will:-	(a)	respond by turning head to the sound of (i) a bell (ii) a rattle
	(b)	be rewarded with tickles for any sound she utters

Feeding

Mary will:—	(a)	take food from a spoon

Toileting

Mary will:-	(a)	be toileted regularly
Teacher will:-		
	(a)	establish a pattern of toilet needs as a base-line for a toilet training programme

Professional involvement with Mary It is well understood that profoundly handicapped children often rightly become the subject of intervention by medical and para-medical services.

In Mary's case these have been chronicled in Table 6 to give some indication of their incidence and effect.

TABLE 6
1977 - 1986

Year	Professional involved	Cause
1977	Physiotherapist	Boots and calipers fitted
1978	Psychologist	Screaming fits and nipping
1978	Physiotherapist	Splints designed and made
1978	Psychologist	Self mutilation
1978	Social Services	Mother wants child at home
1978	Visually Impaired	Spectacles fitted
1978	Physiotherapist	Calipers removed, special footwear changed
1978	Hearing Impaired Service	Hearing aid fitted
1979	Paediatrician	District Handicap Team pass on responsibility to school doctor
1979	Occupational Therapist	Special furniture designed, special eating utensils advised on
1979	Physiotherapist	Special footwear changed
1980	Social Services	Mother demands Mary is returned home
1981	Physiotherapist	Special footwear changed
1981	Hearing impaired service	Hearing aid discontinued
1982	Visually impaired	Spectacles discontinued
1982	Paediatrician	Constipation investigated as cause of distress
1983	Clinical Psychologist	Self-mutilation at children's home
1983	Physiotherapist	Special foot wear discontinued
1984	Psychologist	Self-mutilation
1985	Educational Psychologist	Self mutilation
	Physiotherapist	New splint designed
1985	Social Services	Trampoline purchased for children's home
1986	Clinical Psychologist	Self mutilation at Children's home

If we examine this list in chronological order we see that physiotherapy services were the first involved in providing for her needs and indeed physiotherapy services have continued to provide for her throughout her school life. These consist of a combination of regular manipulations as an aid to her physical development and specialist involvement in the organisation of the manufacture of materials such as footwear, calipers, walking frames, seating aids and splints to prevent self-mutilation.

Psychological intervention has equally proved to be a fairly regular occurrence, as has the provision of assessements to form the basis of teaching programmes. There has also been specialist observation, advice and involvement associated with her self-mutilating behaviours and screaming attacks. This involvement with Mary has entailed the design and monitoring of strategies to reduce head banging and nipping and has been planned in association with clinical psychology services attached to Dr Barnardo's and their care staff.

Medical involvement has been necessary in much the same way. Specialist assessments have had to be made for the fitting of spectacles and hearing aids and these aids have been maintained through the involvement of the Authorities' services for the visually impaired and the hearing impaired. Further specialist involvement occurred when Sarah was the subject of a trial with medication to attempt to ease constipation when this condition was thought to be a possible additional causal factor in the onset of self-mutilating behaviours. Medical services have also contributed a constant review of her general health and development and have dealt with any worries or concerns brought into focus by the children's home who requested that the medical officer for the school assume responsibility for Mary's case.

Nursing services have, of course, been closely linked with this provision. Apart from overseeing general health care, monitoring height and weight levels and administering medicines and drugs, nursing services have since 1982 been administering weekly enemas to relieve constipation.

Social Services involvement again has had two major functions. Firstly in administering the care order sheet they held on Mary and organising the bi-annual reviews involved in such cases and secondly, in dealing with a mother who due to her own mental illness can become problematic. She can, for instance, make no contact with the School for many months and then suddenly want to visit every day, take Mary out of school and even want to take her home. The school and social workers are then presented with the difficult task of trying to help mother while at the same time protecting the interests of the child.

This separation of the role of these different agencies is of course a simplistic view of what actually occurs, for much inter-disciplinary cooperation and involvement is of course necessary and essential. Thus teachers, nurses, doctors, social workers and psychologists, as well as care staff, non- teaching staff and clerical staff all have to be aware of some elements of each others involvement in order to make the child's programme a coherent and comprehensive service.

What has been omitted, because it is taken for granted, is the on-going teaching of programmes which continue throughout the school year and the planning and organisation involved in curriculum development in this very difficult area of profound learning difficulty.

TABLE 7

Mary, Objectives, November 1986

Gross Motor		
Mary will:-	(a)	open doors using handle
	(b)	walk up and down stairs unaided
Fine Motor		
Mary will:-	(a)	pick up ten bricks and place them in a container
	(b)	use touch pad to operate computer/electronic toys/cassette player
Eating		
Mary will:-	(a)	load appropriate amounts of food onto spoon when eating
	(b)	eat lunch within 15 minutes
Drinking		
Mary will:-	(a)	drink unaided from a one-handled cup
	(b)	drink on the verbal prompt 'Drink Sarah
Relaxation		
Mary will:-	(a)	follow relaxation programme Stage 1 using vibrating bed
Eye Contact		
Mary will:-	(a)	make and maintain eye contact for up to three seconds with teacher/aide in one to one situation
Cognitive Skills		
Mary will:-	(a)	retrieve chocolate button from under beaker (object permanence)

To emphasise this point it might be useful to look briefly at the objectives set for Mary (Table 7) at recent case conferences and to compare them with the earlier when she entered school.

It is evident that for ten years education the amount of progress has been small. There is, for example, no speech of any kind and as yet little evidence of cognitive development. It will be appreciated, however, that with such profoundly handicapped children even very small steps forward are sometimes excruciatingly difficult to develop and indeed in some such cases, a criterion of success can be measured in how far the child has not regressed.

The final point that should be made is that during Mary's ten year period in school she has had the services of three psychologists, two physiotherapists, three teachers in charge of unit, three paediatric consultants, two only (surprisingly) social workers etc. It is clear that, in spite of these changes in key personnel, it is the school as an institution that has remained the constant factor in her life, which has acted as a focus for the organisation and direction of treatment and which has collated and collected the knowledge about the child, a knowledge which is so important in planning overall treatment. This aspect of special school organisation can, it is suggested, go some way towards the amelioration of mental handicap.

Finally, in order to broaden the picture, it is useful to examine the influence a school can exert on a population of children over a period of time. Table 8 shows the numbers of children for whom specific programmes designed to meet particular needs were identified and operated in a ten year period.

The figures here show the total number of children who have had specific individual programmes of work designed for them in various categories. Some of these programmes such as the ones designed for children requiring a modified curriculum, a developmental curriculum and a profound and complex learning difficulties curriculum have been of a long-term nature like the one described for Christopher earlier on. Others have been short and designed to deal with events as they have presented themselves such as in Susan's case. Further programmes have been implemented inresponse to requests from parents, doctors and other professionals. The common feature of them all is that they have been designed and implemented to off-set the effects of behavioural difficulties and intellectual impairment associated with mental handicap. Some children will, of course, have been involved in more than one programme.

The figures require little further explanation but they do interestingly reflect the difficulties that children with learning difficulties experience and the decisions that have to be taken to try to remedythem. Some of the difficulties may appear obvious. Toilet

TABLE 8
Numbers of children for whom specific programmes were designed over ten years

	Number
Access to Modified Curriculum	146
Access to Developmental Curriculum	93
Access to Profound Learning Difficulty Curriculum	33
Specific Behaviour Problems	49
Specific Feeding Problems	34
Toiletting	35
Self Help Skills	75
Independence	74
Speech	43
Language	30
Non-verbal Communication	30
Mobility	18

training, feeding and mobility skills clearly make children more acceptable and more functionally operational in the world in which they find themselves. Note though, the large number of behaviour problems dealt with for it is perhaps not so obvious, but nevertheless true, that the child who, because of a serious behaviour problem, is contained within the house due to parental reluctance to take him or her out is surely as handicapped by this as the child with mobility problems. Similarly, the emphasis on the development of self-help and personal skills programmes reflected in those figures indicates how improved performance in these areas can go some way towards off-setting the effects of handicap by enabling greater access to the world we live in.

CONCLUSIONS

In this chapter aspects of school organisation and a small number of case studies of pupils viewed over a ten year period have been brought together. The skills analysis model that the school has used in order to plan its educational provision has allowed for the close and careful recording of pupil progress which has formed the basis of the decisions made at case conferences concerning the review and detailed planning of the experiences that the individual pupil will encounter in the near and distant future. In this way the very different special educational needs of pupils in schools such as West Oaks, to the best of our ability, can be met.

REFERENCE

Gardner, J., Murphy, J., & Crawford, N. (1983) *Skills Analysis Model.* Kidderminster, Worcestershire: British Institute of Mental Handicap.

CHAPTER 10

Secondary Amelioration and Prevention in Mild Mental Handicap*

Stephen Richardson, Helene Koller and Mindy Katz

Department of Pediatrics, Albert Einstein College of Medicine of Yeshiva University, Bronx, NY

INTRODUCTION

The topic of this chapter is enormously complex and allows no easy answers. There are a number of reasons for this complexity. First, definitions used for Mild Mental Handicap (hereafter referred to as MMH) and the ways MMH persons are identified vary from one study to another. Secondly, MMH is the result of interaction between the characteristics of an individual and the social circumstances and conditions in which that individual is placed. With changes in social conditions over time there may be differences in who is identified as MMH. Thirdly, there is wide heterogeneity within a total population of those defined as MMH and contributing to MMH may be genetic factors, brain pathology and social environmental experiences, alone or in combination.

INTERVENTION AND AMELIORATION

Given the points raised in the introductory section of this chapter, intervention strategies will need to be tailored to the particular characteristics of individuals and the general circumstances and conditions in which they live. The major emphasis in amelioration

* This study was supported by the Foundation for Child Development, the William T. Grant Foundation, the National Institute of Child Health and Human Development, Grant No. HD07907, the G. Harold and Leila Y. Mathers Charitable Foundation, the Charitable Trust of Mrs. Abby R. Mauze, the Scottish Home and Health Department, and the Social Science Research Council of the United Kingdom. The author wishes to thank R. Illsley, J. McLaren, and the late G. Horobin of the British Medical Research Council for their help and support.

has been on changing the MMH individual, and less attention has been paid to changing the environment. Many interventions have been directed at some form of training or teaching of MMH persons, and most of the studies have evaluated the effectiveness of the intervention over a relatively short time span. These sometimes only included the MMH individual and sometimes solicited the cooperation of the parents. A pioneer study which focused intervention on the environmental circumstances in which children lived was the "Brooklands" study of Tizard (1964). (See also Clarke and Tizard, 1983.) These are well known so I will not describe them further.

In practice the most widespread intervention with MMH children for purposes of amelioration are programmes of special education in the school system. Despite the widespread use of special education, it has been hard to document the long term effect of these interventions or determine what forms of special education have been more or less effective.

An important consideration in thinking about the secondary amelioration and prevention of MMH is the course of the disorder over time. Do children identified as MMH continue to exhibit noticeable intellectual impairment throughout their lives or do they later become indistinguishable from their peers? An important task for those responsible for children is to prepare them to function effectively as adults. What interventions are needed for the effective socialisation of children? To examine this question it is important to learn about the natural history of MMH young persons through childhood and into adulthood.

Gruenberg (1964) posed a critical question about the socialisation of MMH young people after showing in a number of epidemiological studies that after school leaving age the administrative prevalence of MH drops by approximately one half.

"For this to occur, a large group of people regarded as retarded at 14 must improve in their functioning to the point where people no longer regard them as retarded and also must succeed in escaping their history of earlier unsatisfactory performance... Either these individuals are continuing to be extremely handicapped in later life and are unknown..., or they have stopped being retarded in any real sense at all and do not need any special protection, help or services, in which case one had better change one's concept of what "real" mental retardation "really is"."

The central question he raises is whether or not those mentally retarded children who disappear from adult mental retardation services still remain distinguishable from their peers.

The drop is most likely to occur in the MMH and in our study in Aberdeen, 72% of the MMH received no further MH services between school leaving and age 22. Finding out what happens to

MMH children when they make the transition to adulthood may be a valuable step in seeking clues to amelioration.

It is likely that the MMH children who disappear from further MH services after leaving school will vary across a range of being distinguishable to being indistinguishable in the various roles expected for their sex and age. This variation provides another way of finding clues to amelioration by asking the question, "Why do some do better than other in their post-school lives?" By finding out what kinds of social and biological factors in childhood are associated with or predict different adult histories, we may gain clues about what factors have helped and hindered development. This also provides some basis for selecting which MMH children are in greater need of amelioration and intervention. The information may also suggest whether amelioration should be directed more towards changing the environmental circumstances the child encounters or directed more to changing the personal characteristics of the child. It may suggest that the forms of intervention may be very different, depending on the particular child who is MMH.

The strategy just proposed has been stated in general and conceptual terms. Now I would like briefly to give an example of how we have employed this strategy in a study of MMH. First it is necessary to give a short description of the study design.

The study cohort was derived from the total population born from 1951 through 1955 and resident in Aberdeen, Scotland in 1962. Subjects were defined as MMH if they were administratively classified as such, if they were placed in a special school for retarded children at some time before 16 years of age, and if they scored 50 or higher on intelligence tests administered between ages 7 and 11. Procedures for classification and placement are described elsewhere (Birch et al., 1970).

A follow-up study of the children was carried out as they reached the age of 22. Comprehensive life history interviews were conducted with the young adults and their parents. Records kept by home health visitors (public health nurses), schools, social workers, courts, and adult service facilities provided additional data.

The MMH and most of the comparison subjects left school between 15 and 16 years of age. Approximately two-thirds of the retarded subjects received no further MH services between ages 16 and 22 years, and most of them were gainfully employed during the 6 to 7 year post-school period.

At the time the study population was growing up, Aberdeen had a wide range of industry and a university and was the centre of an agricultural area, a seaport, and a summer resort. The city had a stable population, with no sizable minority or immigrant group. The various agencies, both generic and those serving mentally retarded children, were well run and generally available to all who needed them.

A purpose of the study was to pursue the question posed by Gruenberg and find out what happens to MMH children in the post-school years. How well do they adapt socially? To do this it is important to see how distinguishable they are from non-MH peers with whom they associate in their daily lives as young adults. There are many aspects or domains of their lives in the age period 16-22 after they leave school that are salient. The three domains that will be dealt with here are job histories, peer friendships, and behaviour disturbance. It is appropriate to look at these three separately, because the highest correlation between the measures of these domains is 0.3 for males and 0.23 for females.

Job Histories. It is useful to consider job histories in the context of the conditions of the labour market at the time and place of the study. These conditions can be determined by looking at the cicumstances experienced by the matched comparisons in the study who were not MH. However, of those who make up the matched comparisons, there will be some whose job histories will be predictably different from others. Those comparisons who leave school with academic qualifications that are prerequisite for further education in Universities and Technical Colleges, or for immediate entry into jobs requiring certain academic qualifications will have different job careers from those who leave school without any academic qualifications. We do not need research to know that a MMH person will have a different job history in the years after leaving school than a person who goes to a university.

We felt it more meaningful to look at similarities and differences in job histories between the MMH and the comparisons who left school without academic qualifications. It is these latter who will provide the best information on the circumstances and conditions of that part of the job market the MMH are most likely to encounter. It is the comparisons without academic qualifications at school leaving age who provide the standards against whom we can most appropriately develop measures of deviance or distinguishability and non-deviance or indistinguishability. A further advantage is that the MMH and the comparisons without qualifications both enter the job market at about the same age. A disadvantage of using comparisons without qualifications is that exact matched pairing is lost. For many reasons, we examined the job histories of the males and females separately. A serendipitous finding was that the unqualified female comparisons had a higher mean IQ than the unqualified male comparisons (Females mean IQ=105.3, Males mean IQ=94.5). This was based on a group IQ test at age 9. We also found that the MMH males had a higher mean IQ than the MMH females. These two differences have the effect of bringing the MMH males and comparison males without qualifications closer together and the females further apart. This suggests that MMH females may be more distinguishable than MMH males in the years after leaving school.

Defining Deviance. A difficult question is how empirically to determine whether or not a person may be considered distinguishable or deviant from others in measures used to describe job history. We decided to define as deviant any person whose job history measure was more than one standard deviation below the mean of the comparisons without school qualifications.

Measures of Job History

We chose three measures of job histories:

1) *Time employed.* The percentage of time employed in the open job market between leaving school and age 22. Percentage was used because the young people's age at leaving school depended largely on their birth date and could vary by as much as a year.

2) *Unemployment.* The percentage of time in the job market the young person was unemployed. This removes from consideration time spent out of the job market engaged in such activities during working hour time as being a housewife, being in adult MH services, or periods away from work because of sickness, injury or being in prison.

3) *Job Turnover.* This was the number of jobs held per year employed.

These measures describe three aspects of a job history which may be judged important by society. They do not include the kind of job held, eg, level of skill required to perform the job because it does not make a person distinguishable to be in an unskilled job. We looked at the three measures in terms of whether individuals were deviant on 1, 2 or 3 of the measures.

Table 1 shows that 43% of the MMH males and 28% of the females were not deviant on any of the three measures of job history. At the other extreme, 3% of the MMH males and 5% of the MMH females were deviant on all three measures. A further 15% and 20% of the MMH males and females had never been in open employment and had largely been instead in adult MH services. These latter young people were the most deviant of all. To relate these findings to Gruenberg's question of whether MH children become indistinguishable from peers who are not MH after leaving school, nearly half of the MMH males and about a quarter of the females became indistinguishable on these three measures of job history.

TABLE 1

MMH males and females who were and were not deviant**
in job history measures of % time employed.
unemplyment and job turnover

	MMH		Comparison	
	without school qualifications			
	Male	Female	Male	Female
Not deviant on any of three measures	38 (43%)	18 (28%)	24 (73%)	13 (68%)
Deviant on % time employed only	8 (9%)	14 (22%)	2 (6%)	2 (11%)
Deviant on unemployment only	4 (4%)	3 (5%)	2 (6%)	1 (5%)
Deviant on turnover only	2 (2%)	3 (5%)	3 (9%)	2 (11%)
Total deviant on 1 measure	14 (15%)	20 (32%)	7 (21%)	5 (27%)
Deviant on any 2 of 3 measures	21 (24%)	11 (17%)	1 (3%)	0
Deviant on all 3 measures	3 (3%)	3 (5%)	1 (3%)	1 (5%)
Never in open employment (employed less than 1 month)	13 (15%)	13 (20%)	0	0
Total	89	65	33	19

**Deviance was defined as having a score on a variable that was more than one standard deviation below the mean obtained from comparisons without school leaving qualifications.

Peer Friendships. A second adult domain of daily living is peer friendships. These may be of particular importance to young adults because they need to gain some emancipation from their parents and families of origin and take over the initiative in making friends.Our measure of peer friendships was based on answers to a series of questions which asked about friends in a range of different settings: neighbourhood, work place, leisure time activities, and continuation of school friendships. While the questions did not confine answers to the same sex friendships, the answers were mostly about friends of the same sex as the informant. Our definition of deviant or distinguishable in this domain was socialising with a peer other than a relative less than once a month, or having no peer friends. We termed this category "isolated", and as Table 2 reveals it consisted of the 26% of the male MMH and 35% of the female MMH population. Those who were in adult MH services were less often "isolated" than those in the job market. The most isolated were the females not in adult MH services (Koller et al. 1989).

Behaviour Disturbance Between Ages 16 and 22

For each study subject we assessed the presence and severity of behaviour disturbance based on the amount of time and the degree to which the disturbance impaired the individual's ability to function as expected, and evidence of concern about the behaviour by the person him or herself, the family or some authority. Overall severity was rated on a five-point scale with 3 being moderate and 5

TABLE 2
Peer friendships of MMH and Comparison males and females

	MMH		Comparison	
	Male	Female	Male	Female
Socialises with peers	49 (74%)	36 (65%)	21 (64%)	14 (93%)
Isolated	17 (26%)	19 (35%)	4 (16%)	1 (7%)

TABLE 3
Overall Behaviour Disturbances in the Post-School Period (16-22)

	MMH		Comparison	
	Male	Female	Male	Female
Not Deviant				
None (0)	29 (32%)	31 (48%)	15 (45%)	16 (84%)
Mild to Mild Moderate (1-2)	28 (31%)	12 (18%)	13 (39%)	1 (5%)
Deviant				
Moderate to Severe (3-5)	34 (37%)	22 (34%)	5 (15%)	2 (11%)
Total	91	65	33	19

being severe. We judged study subjects to be deviant if their disturbance was scored in the 3-5 range. Persons so judged would be likely to come to the clinical attention of a professional. Table three shows that 37% of the male MMH and 34% of the female MMH were deviant. For both MMH males and females there was more deviant behaviour than for comparisons of the same sex (Koller et al. 1982)

Deviance across the Three Measures. Because of the low correlations between the three domains of the young people's lives after leaving school, we looked to see how many of the MMH were not deviant on any of the three measures. Table four reveals that 32% of the males and 15% of the females who were MMH met the criteria of non-deviance, or of being indistinguishable. At the other extreme, 6% of the MMH males and 16% of the MMH females were deviant on all three measures.

TABLE 4
Amount of Deviance Across the Three Adult Domains of Job Histories, Peer Relations and Behaviour

	MMH		Comparison	
	Male	Female	Male	Female
Number of Measures on which deviant				
0	21 (32%)	8 (15%)	16 (64%)	8 (57%)
1	23 (35%)	23 (42%)	4 (16%)	6 (43%)
2	18 (27%)	15 (27%)	4 (16%)	1 (7%)
3	4 (6%)	9 (16%)	1 (4%)	0 (0%)
Total	66	55	25	14

These analyses provide a partial answer to the question raised by Gruenberg that gave much of the impetus to our work. The results show that there is a good distribution of the MMH cases across the measures we have used, from indistinguishable to distinguishable. This distribution enables us to ask our second major question, "Why do some young people do better than others in the various domains of their post-school lives?". If we can predict the level of adult functioning from measures derived from their childhood histories, these predictions may give clues to secondary prevention or amelioration during childhood. This is one of the goals of our work and we are still developing measures needed to do this task adequately. For purposes of illustration, I will give a preliminary analysis. For the independent variables of measures of childhood we used six measures. The first three deal with individual characteristics.

1) IQ at ages 8-10.
2) The overall severity measure of behaviour disturbance as well as separate categories rating the severity of each of four types of disturbance.
3) Evidence of brain pathology based on a paediatric neurological examination.

The next two measures deal more with the environment.

4) Social class of the head of the household when the young person was aged 8-10.

5) A measure of family stability.
   The final measure deals with the individual's characteristics in interaction with the school environment.
6) The history of special education based on age classified as MH and type of facility in which young person was placed.

For the dependent variables of adult outcomes we used the three adult domains we have described. Using multiple regression analyses we were unable to obtain a significant R^2 between the childhood measures and either job histories or peer relations. For adult behaviour disturbance, there was a significant relationship which accounted for 29% of the variance for males. The female prediction was not significant. For predicting adult behaviour disturbance, we then added as an independent variable, childhood behaviour disturbance. This improved the prediction for males to an R^2 of .41 and the females R^2 to .29 which was not significant. The factors which contributed to the prediction of adult behaviour disturbance for males were higher IQ, being classified at a later age, family instability, and childhood behaviour disturbance. For females the childhood factors were behaviour disturbance and lower social class.

It appears that the adult domain best predicted deals more with an individual characteristic, while the domains of job history and peer relations, which have a greater interaction component with social environmental factors, are more difficult to predict. Our next steps will be to develop more independent childhood variables and more dependent adult measures. We will also use more complex analytical models of multiple independent variables to predict multiple dependent outcomes in adulthood.

To return to our first purpose of finding out what happens to MMH children after leaving school, there is another approach which may yield clues to secondary prevention and amelioration and that is by a more detailed examination of social and physical environments experienced by the MMH young persons. This approach may be illustrated by examining job histories. We know that the majority of jobs held by the MMH are unskilled, manual jobs, and in these jobs there is wide variation in the time stayed in a particular job, degree of satisfaction with a job, and reasons for leaving jobs. We have begun looking at the conditions that exist in the wide range of unskilled manual jobs held by the study population. This examination includes:

1. The physical environment in which the work is carried out, e.g. amount of wet, cold, noise, smell, dust, and whether indoors or outdoors.
2. The physical demands and hazards of the job.
3. The conditions of employment: hours of work, steadiness of employment, and amount of pay.

4. The conditions of supervision.
5. Relationship with work mates.

By examining these conditions in unskilled jobs where employees tend to stay and like the work, and those where employees do not stay and dislike the work, we can learn something about the situations of work which may provide a basis for changing some of the working conditions to make them more attractive. This approach differs from most past efforts at amelioration, which focused on the individual characteristics of the person with MMH.

CONCLUSION

These preliminary analyses reinforce the initial contention of the paper that secondary amelioration and prevention in MMH is difficult and complex. It suggests that amelioration in childhood needs to be focussed on both individual characteristics of the child and the social conditions of upbringing. Mildly mentally handicapped children with behaviour disturbance appear to be at heightened risk of encountering difficulties as young adults suggesting that amelioration of the disturbance may have important beneficial consequences. Children from unstable backgrounds also appear to be at risk of later difficulties. Improvement of their conditions of upbringing also appear to be a strategic focus for amelioration. Turning to young adults, if we can determine the kinds of working conditions felt by the MMH to be congenial and uncongenial these maysuggest ways of making working environments more congenial.

REFERENCES

Birch, H. G., Richardson, S. A., Baird, D., Horobin, G. & Illsley, R. (1970). *Mental Subnormality in the community: A clinical and epidemiologic study*. Baltimore: Williams and Wilkins.

Clarke, A. D. B. & Tizard, B. (Eds.) (1983) *Child development and social policy. The life and work of Jack Tizard* (Ch. 5). Leicester: The British Psychological Society.

Gruenberg, E. M. (1964) Epidemiology. In H. A. Stevens and R. Heber (Eds.) *Mental Retardation*. Chicago: University of Chicago Press.

Koller, H., Richardson, S. A., Katz, M. & McLaren, J. (1982) Behaviour disturbance in childhood and the early adult years in populations who were and were not mentally retarded. *Journal of Preventive Psychiatry*, **1:4,** 453-468.

Koller, H., Richardson, S. A., & Katz, M. (1989) *Peer relationships of mildly retarded young adults living in the community.*

Tizard, J. (1964) *Community Services for the Mentally Handicapped*. Oxford: Oxford University Press.

CHAPTER 11

Portage Guide to Early Education: Partnership With Parents and Cross-Cultural Aspects

Peter Sturmey

Department of Psychology, University of Birmingham, Birmingham, UK

INTRODUCTION

The Portage Guide to Early Education (Shearer and Shearer, 1972) is a home-based, skills teaching approach to the prevention and amelioration of a wide range of handicapping conditions. It consists of three main elements. Firstly, parents teach their children at home with weekly visits from their Home Visitor. This person assists in selecting goals, and trains the parents to teach by modelling and feedback. Secondly, there is a package of teaching materials which includes a development checklist (Bluma et al., 1976), an Instructor's manual for the Home Visitors (Boyd, Stauber and Bluma, 1977), and an inventory of parent teaching behaviours (Boyd and Stauber, 1977). Thirdly, there is a hierarchical model of service delivery consisting of Home Visitors monitoring progress in the home. Supervisors (usually educational or clinical psychologists) meet weekly with Home Visitors to monitor goal plans, liaise concerning referrals. A Management Team meets every 3 to 6 months which monitors the entire service and liaises with other agencies.

This service, which originated in a rural part of the United States, has now been developed and expanded in many ways. It has been implemented widely in both the United Kingdom (Cameron, 1987) and Japan (Yamaguchi, 1986) where national Portage associations exist. It has also been used in Peru (Jesian et al., 1979; Shearer and Loftin, 1984), New Zealand (Painter, 1986), India (Kholi, 1986), Gaza Strip (Shearer and Ghazaleh, 1986) and Iceland (Cunningham, *personal communication*). It has been used not only in the home but also in nurseries (Clements et al., 1982). A wide variety of materials have been employed to augment those specificallly developed for Portage.

Since its inception twenty years ago the political and ideological climate and the pattern of services for handicapped and at risk children has shifted substantially. The greater emphasis on accountability and evaluation has given rise to an increase in evaluations of early intervention generally. A recent series of meta-analyses has identified over 400 evaluative studies of early intervention (White and Casto, 1985). A number of long-term evaluations of the effects of early intervention into late adolescence and early adulthood have become available (Lazar and Darlington, 1982; Gray, Ramsey and Klaus, 1982).

In this chapter the outcome literature on Portage with respect to IQ and skills gained which has been discussed in more detail elsewhere will be briefly summarised (Sturmey and Crisp, 1986; Spitz, 1986b). Two aspects of evaluation will be examined in more detail - parent participation and cross- cultural aspects of Portage. It will be argued that attempts to ascertain parental participation have been both empirically weak, in collecting poor and ambiguous data, and conceptually naive, in failing to opt for an interactional/ecological model of matching client and programme characteristics. The exporting of Portage into a wide range of cultural contexts raises a number of issues. The different patterns of aetiologies found across cultures, the changes in test norms and referral practices, the differences in implicit models of development and differing attitudes to the nature of infancy and the handicapped infant in particular all raise potential difficulties and suggest future developments of Portage in a foreign land.

CHANGES IN IQ AND SKILLS

Changes in IQ are the most common outcome measure in the early intervention literature (Casto and White, 1985) and is thus the common metric for comparing studies. Indeed, attempts to raise intelligence have been undertaken for 200 years (Spitz, 1986a). In their original evaluative study Shearer and Shearer (1972) showed that children with an average initial IQ of 75 gained an average of 13 months mental age in an eight month period whilst receiving the service. Multiple replications of this effect have been demonstrated with a wide range of children ranging from multiply handicapped to disadvantaged on at least eight sites (Cochran and Shearer, 1987; Shearer and Loftin, 1984; Pennington, 1972). In Japan Yamaguchi (1986) has shown increases in the developmental quotients in both

Down's Syndrome and non-Down's Syndrome infants. The average gain was 3.5 points on the Tsarimotor Developmental Test. This should be judged against the likelihood that the IQ may decline substantially for both Down's Syndrome and non-Down's Syndrome children without intervention (Ludlow and Allen, 1979). A similar effect for Down's Syndrome infants in a Portage project has been shown elsewhere (Woods et al., 1984). These studies are highly suggestive that Portage raised the IQ's of children who would probably have otherwise shown declines in IQ. However, the lack of control groups in all these studies can not exclude the possibility that at least some of these effects were due to non-specific effects of Portage (e.g. reactive repeated assessment, generally orienting parents to a more positive view of their children).

Only two studies, evaluating the Portage model, which have studied changes in IQ have included control groups. Jesian et al. (1979) studied changes in mental age in their study of Portage in Peru. In their group of rural children the experimental group (90 families) gained an average 12 months mental age on the Leitner International Performance Scale compared to only 4 months mental age on average in the no treatment control group (45 families). Differences on most of the subscales of the McCarthy Scales of Children's Abilities were also statistically significant both for the groups of rural children described above and also for a sample of urban ghetto children. This study is impressive in its large gains in mental age in groups of children exposed to multiple cumulating risks for mental handicap. A second experimental study failed to replicate such dramatic changes in IQ. Sandow and Clarke (1978) and Sandow et al. (1981) compared changes in Cattell mental ages in 3 groups of children. Two groups received home visits either every two weeks or every eight weeks and the third group was a no treatment control group. At the end of 3 years of the service there was no statistically significant difference between the groups. However, it should be noted that all of the children in this group had established biological handicaps (Mean Cattell IQ at pretest was 43) and that there was a statistically non-significant trend in favour of the two treatment groups. The results of changes in intelligence are, in broad outline, similar to those reported in other attempts to raise intelligence (Spitz, 1986a, 1986b; Lazar and Darlington, 1982; Bricker et al., 1984).

Skills development. A second approach to evaluating changes in the child's behaviour has been to report the proportion of goals set and achieved during the home visits. The results of some of these studies are shown in Table 1.

Although these results appear promising it is unclear if they provide data on the outcome or the implementation of Portage

(Clements et al., 1982). Further, given the extremely rapid acquisition of goals reported in some studies (Daly, 1980) it would seem possible that in some circumstances Home Visitors either set very fine goals of dubious immediate functional significance, use excessively liberal criteria or teach parents to elicit behaviours from their children which are already in their repertoire.

TABLE 1
Outcome studies measuring the proportion of weekly goals set that were achieved

Study	% Goals Achieved
Clements et al. (1982)	58%
Smith et al. (1977)	82%
Daly (1980)	84%
Cole (1982)	91%
Shearer & Shearer (1972)	91%
Frederikson & Harran (1986)	90.9%
Kirklees Project (cited in Jewell & Brookes, 1986)	80%

PARTNERSHIP WITH PARENTS

The notion of 'partnership with parents' is now highly fashionable and has been enshrined in both British and American legislation (Wolfendale, 1985; The Education Act, 1981). Reports of Portage make frequent reference to this phrase (Daly et al., 1985). Parents become involved with Portage principally through teaching their children, although active efforts are made to integrate them within the National Portage Association and its annual conferences. 'Partnership with parents' and the views of parents have been ascertained firstly by self-reports of satisfaction and related constructs, some of which attempted to include measures of maternal distress. Secondly, data concerning compliance with the service has been published. Finally, Cameron (1986) has reported some data on complaints concerning Portage.

The most commonly used methodology has been to use *ad hoc* rating scales developed specifically for the purpose. Smith et al., (1977) reported that for the items 'The home visitor has dealt satisfactorily with any problems I have had regarding activity charts with regard to 1) carrying out the activity, 2) carrying out correction procedure and 3) filling in the record chart' all mothers (n = 12) rated all three items as 'usually' or 'always'. Similar data are presented for general satisfaction with the Home Visitors' advice (Smith et al., 1977), child progress, recommending the service to other parents (Daly, 1980), global satisfaction (Land, 1985; Myatt, 1983; Jewell and Brookes, 1984) confidence with interacting with and teaching the child, knowledge of child development (Jewell and Brookes, 1984) and satisfaction with training in Portage (Frederikson and Haran, 1986).

Despite this generally positive endorsement of Portage by parents (almost always mothers) these data are highly ambiguous. Almost all studies do not use established instruments and consequently lack reliability and validity studies. Typically the number of subjects is very small and none include a control group or comparison with other services. Myatt (1983) used the Judson Self-rating Scales which gives four subscale totals (attitude to self, perception of child, attitude to child and attitudes to professionals) and a total score. Using a pre-post comparison it appeared that an average mother's attitude improved. Other studies have also reported decreases in self reported depression by mothers during Portage (Burden, 1980; Holland and Noaks, 1980). Again, because of the lack of control group it is unclear whether these changes would have occurred without Portage as part of the normal process of accommodation to having a handicapped child in the family. Further, since the data on the pre-scores appear to have been collected retrospectively in Myatt (1983) the role of demand characteristics may have been important. Compliance with the service may also be regarded as an indirect measure of satisfaction. As noted in the previous section, reported compliance with teaching is often high (See Table 1; Smith et al., 1977). Similarly, although most services do not report drop out, those that do have found dropout to be less than 15% (Jesian et al., 1979). One exception to this was Kholi and Datta's (1984) study of Portage in India who found that five out of ten mothers were unwilling to attempt home teaching, although they were willing to bring their children to a centre. Compliance with home teaching may vary substantially with the resources and demands placed upon the mother (Dunst et al., 1985).

Finally, Cameron (1986) reported on complaints made at Portage review meetings over a 9 year period. During this time 151 parties had participated. Over three quarters of complaints were not about Portage. Ninety-two percent of complaints about Portage were from professionals and 93 per cent of parents' complaints were about non-Portage services. However, no control data are presented. (For example, it may be the case that parents complain to Portage about paediatricians and to paediatricians about Portage!).

Thus, whilst a variety of aspects of partnership with parents have been explored, the data in this matter are relatively restricted and compromised by numerous unresolved methodological and conceptual flaws. Perhaps more important has been the assumption that uniformly high ratings of satisfaction, high rates of compliance and low rates of complaints are necessarily desirable. The families of mentally handicapped pre-schoolers are highly variable with a wide range of needs, strengths and resources. Child characteristics such as additional handicaps and developmental status (Barna, Bidder, Gray, Clements and Gardner, 1982; Bidder, Hewitt and Gray, 1982) may be associated with rate of progress in home-based teaching and parents' preferences for different home and centre-based services (Wishart, Bidder and Gray, 1980). Maternal characteristics such as general education (Cullen, Cronk, Pueschel, Schnell and Reed, 1981), knowledge of behaviour therapy (Clark, Baker and Heifetz, 1982) social class (Clark et al. 1982; Dumas and Wahler, 1983), depression (Greist, Forehand and Wells, 1981) and social isolation (Dumas and Wahler,1983) may all mediate the outcome of early interaction. Similarly, characteristics of the entire family such as resources available (Dunst and Leet, 1989), family support (Dunst, Jenkins and Trivette, 1984) act in a complex manner to mediate multiple outcomes such as child status, family well-being and styles of mother-child interaction (Dunst et al. 1986).

Up to now, the evaluations of parental satisfaction with Portage have been based on a 'main effects' model. That is, certain outcomes are deemed desirable irrespective of mediating variables such as those delineated above. A series of recent papers have strongly argued for individualization of parental participation in early intervention (Turnbull and Turnbull, 1982). Such participation might range from active involvement in the education of their child, to being actively consulted, to being informed and to opting out of early intervention without guilt (Macmillan and Turnbull, 1983; Winston and Turnbull, 1981). Further, the optimum degree of involvement may vary from time to time. In this model mediating variables are fully recognized as important in both determining optimum services to the child and family but also in the evaluation of early intervention. Thus, this interactional approach would perceive low ratings of satisfaction, low compliance and high complaints as being characteristic of any form of early intervention dependent upon a host of mediating variables. Ecological models of early intervention now emphasise the important role of a wide range of mediating variables and recommend intervening within the entire network of the family rather than targetting an isolated individual (Dunst, 1985; Barrera and Rosenbaum, 1986).

Casting the evaluations of partnership with parents in this framework it seems unexpected that such uniform outcomes have been found. A number of explanations are possible. It may be that the instruments used have been insensitive due to contamination from response acquiescence and demand characteristics. Alternatively, selection of families - by self-selection, differential referral to the service by other agencies of 'suitable' families, selection by the service itself, or differential drop-out — may account for the uniform outcomes of these studies. It is worth noting that no study to date has reported on any aspect of differential selection or drop-out from Portage.

If parents of handicapped pre-schoolers are to enter into partnership with professionals greater care must be taken in the evaluation of parents' resources and needs. Given that families are so diverse it is unlikely that any one form of early intervention could uniformly serve all of them with equal efficacy and satisfaction. Failure to recognise this is a failure in the partnership with parents.

CROSS-CULTURAL ASPECTS

As noted earlier Portage was developed 20 years ago in an American rural area to serve a group of predominantly at risk and mildly mentally handicapped preschoolers (Shearer and Shearer, 1972; Shearer and Loftin, 1984; Cochran and Shearer, 1984). As such it falls broadly within the *zeitgeist* of the Headstart-type of programme (Lazar and Darlington, 1982). The implicit model of mental handicap was that these children were at risk of underfunctioning due to lack of environmental opportunity to learn (Ramey and Suarez, 1985; Barrera and Rosenbaum, 1986). Consequently, Portage matched this need by showing parents how to stimulate and teach their children before substantial intellectual delay occurred (Pennington, 1972). Exporting Portage across national boundaries and time raises a number of important issues. These include the translation of the materials into new languages, the development of new norms for the developmental checklist, the matching of a skills-teaching approach to the local spectrum of aetiologies and the matching of this approach to early intervention with the local culture and belief system.

The Portage materials have now been translated into over 15 languages (Cameron, *personal communication*) and this presents a number of potential difficulties. The correspondence between American, English and European languages is relatively good, but the translation of non-European languages may require the insertion of some items and the deletion of others which have no clear mutual correspondence. Similarly, words and phrases referring to certain social behaviour may also not be appropriate in all cultures. Yamaguchi (1986) noted that in the Japanese translation of the developmental checklist (Bluma et al., 1976) the items 'uses the articles *the, a* in speech' and 'slides on a sled' were eliminated as were others. However, the phrase 'uses articles *ne, yo* in speech' was added. Further, in multi-lingual societies the use of the culturally dominant language may carry with it many connotations for minority groups which may prejudice the viability of the intervention in some cultures (Syed, 1986). Translation of checklists is better thought of as adaption rather than as literal translation (Syed, 1986).

The ages at which certain behaviours are typically achieved may vary widely across cultures. Syed (1986) noted that in both native Indian families and immigrant Indian families in England self-reliance is not emphasized in child rearing. A non-handicapped child may sleep with its parents, be bathed, fed and dressed until five years of age. Departures from developmental sequences established in one culture may occur when cultures are compared. For example, Deer and Kelly (1982) found that the order in which conservation of number, quantity and length were achieved was different in children in East Java compared to Western Europe. The potentially large discrepancies in norms and sequences of development have important implications for the implementation of Portage in different cultures. The selection of goals, the order in which tasks are taught and criteria for referral and discharge may all be substantially affected by these phenomena.

The spectrum of aetiologies of mental handicap vary radically from one country to another. In the third world global malnutrition (Richardson, 1985) specific nutritional deficits (Hetzel, 1986) and infectious disease are much more important than in the developed world. Prevention of mental handicap is much more closely related to the health of the community than to education. When Jesian et al. (1979) introduced Portage into Peru the curriculum guide was extended to include 'health, hygiene and personal safety objectives' (p.67). The Home Visitor, as well as assisting the mother in skills teaching, also discussed nutrition, health, hygiene, economic menu planning, food preparation and vaccination. Such flexibility is advantageous. However, where specific aetiological factors can be identified and readily remediated (e.g. Hetzel, 1986) home-based skills teaching may not marry closely to the cause of mental handicap and may be relatively expensive compared to alternative methods of intervention. Indeed, Jesian et al. (1979) noted that "...in areas of extreme poverty, food supplements may be necessary" (p.68).

Perhaps the most interesting, pervasive and subtle influences on the acceptability (and perhaps efficacy) of Portage in non- Western cultures are the values, attitudes and behaviours of the culture into which it is implemented. Syed (1986), an educational psychologist working with Asian families in London and brought up in Gujarat, discusses in detail some of the obvious and less obvious cultural differences which affect using Portage with Asian families. The extended family, and in particular several adult women rather than the mother alone, bringing up children is highlighted. Syed also noted that the attitudes to children in general may undermine an intervention which emphasizes independence in children. Syed noted that traditional child training and socialization emphasizes observation rather than direct instruction as the normal method of learning. A child is often seen as '... a gift of the gods, to be welcomed, appreciated and even indulged in the first few years of life - [this view] is so deeply rooted in the Hindu world-image that it influences every aspect of adults' relationship with children'. This more indulgent approach to child rearing has received empirical support from cross-cultural studies of parenting in America, Japan and India (Sinha, 1985). Syed notes that in many ways Portage may be imperfectly tuned to the Asian culture. For example, immigrant Asian families in Britain may be extremely unfamiliar with the 'new services' currently available for families of mentally handicapped children which may have no ready correspondence in their own culture. Bardsley and Perkins (1985) have also reported on working with Asian families and they have found broadly similar findings to the observations made by Syed (1986). They also note the difficulty in working with parents using translators for twelve families speaking three different languages. They also found that, compared to non-Asian families, Asian families had mixed expectations of the likely efficacy of teaching, poorer knowledge of the nature and implications of their child's handicap and fewer materials in the home for teaching.

A large number of studies have been carried out comparing child rearing practices in different cultures (e.g. Landau, 1982; Keller et al., 1984) which may have bearing upon the acceptability of Portage in non-Western cultures. Since there is now a national Portage Association in Japan (Yamaguchi, 1986) comparisons between Japanese and American cultures will be used to illustrate this point. Quirk, Ciittone et al. (1986), in a study of self-reported values of parents, found that Japanese mothers were most likely to value their children's health, activity, affect and cultural awareness, whereas American parents were most likely to value self-confidence, creativity, morality and productivity in their children. These values reflect the importance attached in Japan to *amae* - personal discipline, loyalty and afiliation with others - during childhood, whereas in America the dominant cultural values are those of individualism, autonomy and competition. Such differences have been replicated elsewhere and continue into school (Hess, Kasiwagi et al. 1980; Kasiwagi et al., 1982).

Cultural differences in child rearing practices have also been found in observational studies of parenting which may have implications for a home-based, skills teaching approacah to early intervention. Otaki et al. (1986) attempted to replicate differences in parenting practices between Japanese and American parents observed by Caudill and Weinstein (1969) almost 20 years earlier. They observed 30 American and 52 Japanese mother-infant dyads from middle-class homes. The infants were three to four months old. Non- participant observations were carried out during two separate morning and afternoon sessions. Japanese mothers spent more time with their infants and American mothers were more likely to actively position their infants. These differences were broadly similar to those found 20 years earlier by Caudill and Weinstein despite the presumed filtering of American ideas into Japanese culture during that time. This study has implications concerning both the amount of time available to mothers to teach their children as well as opportunities to generalize from formal teaching. Shand and Kosawa (1985) replicated the finding that American mothers had a more active,stimulating style of interacting with non-handicapped infants than Japanese mothers. The natural style of management upon which a behavioural approach is grafted also differs both in terms of how actively parents manage their children (Otaki et al. 1986) but also their predisposition to the imperatives and authority (Sinha, 1986) during management. It should be noted that the readability of Portage materials may present difficulties for some British parents (Sturmey and Crisp, 1986). In parts of third world countries illiteracy may be a major obstacle in a style of intervention which often uses reading materials and requires them to record on a daily basis (Kholi, 1986).

CONCLUSIONS

Portage has been implemented in a wide range of radically different contexts from that in which it was developed. These contexts have varied in the types of handicapping conditions, the range of families, settings and cultures. It is clearly both robust and amenable to local modification.

'Partnership with parents' is a popular slogan. However, the notion of individualized parental participation has not yet been fully acknowledged. A variety of services, such as bereavement counselling, family counselling, intensive training in behavioural techniques and nutrition and health advice modules, have been added on to the home-based, skills- teaching approach depending upon the needs of the families and children. Nevertheless, the option for families to withdraw from Portage, select other early intervention services or use Portage only at certain times has not been fully and explicitly recognised. Turnbull and Turnbull (1982) discuss some of the assumptions made in advocating that parents should teach the handicapped infant some of the skills they require. Parents as teachers assume that they wish to teach their child, that they are able and should teach their child, that they are willing to receive training to do so and that the child will benefit from such teaching. In order to emphasize the individuality of parents' responses to home-based teaching they cite two contrasting reactions to withdrawal of services (Winston and Turnbull, 1981).

> "I cried for two months last spring - I knew what was going to happen. I didn't know it would be as drastic. I was hoping that there would be some type of parental support but it just didn't happen."
>
> "It is definitely refreshing. You feel really bad for the professionals who want to help you but don't know how. You know, the psychologists and social workers have this concept that every parent with a handicapped child wants to talk about it all the time. That's garbage!"

The notion of individualized parental participation fits well with the recent development of ecological models of intervention (Dunst, 1985; Dunst et al., 1985; Barrera and Rosenbaum, 1986). Such ecological models recognize that early intervention is only one of several powerful influences on development of a handicapped or at risk child. Factors such as the social network of the family, its resources and needs other than those of the index child, are paramount in influencing the later development of both the index child and the entire family (Dunst et al., 1985). Within this framework early intervention targets not only the skills of the index child through teaching but also intervenes in assisting parents to increase and control resources, utilize and develop their social support network to the full, including a wide array of educational, health and social service modules available to the family (Dunst, 1985). Further, it emphasized multi-disciplinary work, and may include a variety of centre-based services including social activities for the family, libraries and information (Barrera and Rosenbaum, 1986).

The influences on Portage of non-western cultures are likely to be diverse, subtle and difficult to ascertain. Further, investigations of the match or mismatch in different cultures are required. Portage is an achievement-oriented programme, typically dependent upon the mother. It is now implemented in countries where educational aspects of prevention may not be as important as those related to health, very different circumstances from those obtaining in Portage, Wisconsin in 1969. The expectations of parents and children in particular may also differ substantially and affect the suitability of this approach in new contexts.

REFERENCES

Bardsley, J. & Perkins, E. (1985) Portage with Asian families in central Birmingham. In Daly, B., Addington, J., Kerfoot, S. and Sigston, A. (Eds.) *Portage : the importance of parents.* Windsor, Berkshire: NFER-Nelson.

Barna,S., Bidder,R.T., Gray,O.P., Clements,J. & Garner,S. (1982) The progress of developmentally delayed pre-school children in a home-visiting scheme, *Child: Care, Health and Development,* **6,** 157-164.

Barrera, M. & Rosenbaum, P. (1986). The transactional model of early home intervention. *Infant Mental Health Journal,* **7,** 112-131.

Bidder,R.T., Hewitt, K.E., & Gray, O.P. (1982) Evaluation of teaching methods in a home-based training scheme for developmentally delayed pre-school children, *Child: Care, Health and Development,* **9,** 1-12.

Bluma, S., Shearer, M., Frohman, A. & Hillard, J. (1976). *Portage Guide to Early Education Manual.* Revised Edition. Portage, Wisconsin: CESA-12.

Boyd, R.D. & Stauber, K.A. (1977). Parental Behaviour Inventory. In Boyd, R.D., Stauber, K.A. and Bluma, S.M. *Instructor's Manual. Portage Parent Program.* Portage, Wisconsin: CESA-12.

Boyd, R.D., Stauber, K.A. & Bluma, S.M. (1977) *Instructor's Manual. Portage Parent Program.* Portage, Wisconsin: CESA-12.

Bricker, D., Bailey, E. & Bruder, M.B. (1984) The efficacy of early intervention and the handicapped infant. A wise or wasted resource. *Advances in Developmental and Behavioural Pediatrics,* **5,** 374- 423.

Burden, R. (1980) Measuring the effects of stress on mothers of handicapped infants : must depression always follow? *Child: Care, Health and Development,* **6,** 111-127.

Cameron, S. (1986) They can't mean us: criticisms and comments about Portage. In Hedderley, R. and Jennings, K (Eds) *Portage: progress, problems and possibilities.* Windsor, Berkshire: NFER-Nelson.

Caudill, W.A. & Weinstein, H. (1969) Maternal care and infant behaviour in Japan and America. *Psychiatry* **32,** 12- 43.

Clark,D.B., Baker,B.L. & Heifetz, L.J. (1982) Behavioural training for parents of mentally handicapped children: prediction of outcome, *American Journal of Mental Deficiency,* **87,** 14-19.

Clements, J., Evans, C., Jones, C. Osbourne, K., & Upton. A (1982) Evaluation of a home-based language training programme with severely mentally handicapped children. *Behaviour Research and Therapy,* **20,** 243-249.

Clements, J.C., Smith, J., Spain, B. & Watkeys, J. (1982) A preliminary investigation on the use of the Portage system in day nursery settings. *Child: Care, Health and Development,* **8,** 123-131.

Cochran, D.C. & Shearer, D.E. (1984) The Portage model for home teaching. In Daine, S.C., Bellamy, C.T. and Wilcox, B. (Eds.) *Human services that work: from innovation to standard practice.* Baltimore: Brookes.

Cullen, S.M., Cronk, C.E., Pueschel, S.M., Schnell,R R., & Reed,R.B. (1981) Social development and feeding milestones of young Down's Syndrome infants, *American Journal of Mental Deficiency,* **85,** 410-415

Daly, B. (1980) *Evaluation of Portage home teaching pilot project for preschool handicapped children. June 1979 - June 1980. A summary of report No. P/S 02.*

Daly, B., Addington, J., Kerfoot, S. & Sigston, A. (1985) *Portage: the importance of parents.* Windsor, Berkshire: NFER-Nelson.

Deer, C.E., & Kelly, M. (1982) Piagetian tasks for curriculum construction in Java using sequence analysis. *Journal of Cross-Cultural Psychology* **13,** 217-227.

Dumas, J.E., & Wahler,R.G. (1983) Predictions of treatment outcome in parent training: mother insularity and socioeconomic disadvantage *Behavioral Assessment,* **5,** 301-313.

Dunst, C.J. (1985) Rethinking early intervention. *Analysis and Intervention in Developmental Disabilities* **5,** 165-201.

Dunst, C.J., Jenkins, V. & Trivette, C.M. (1984) The Family Support Scale : reliability and validity. *Journal of Individual, Family and Community Wellness,* **1,** 45-52.

Dunst, C.J. & Leet, H.E. (1987) Meaning the adequacy of resources in households with young children. *Child: Care, Health and Development,* **13.** 111-125.

Dunst, C.J., Trivette, C.M. & Cross, A.H. (1986) Mediating influences of social support: personal, family and child. *American Journal of Mental Deficiency,* **90,** 403-417.

Education Act (1981) London: HMSO.

Frederikson, N. & Haran, H. (1986) Portage evaluation and re-evaluation: a day nursery project. *Educational Psychology in Practice,* **1,** 159-169.

Gray, S.W., Ramsey, B.K. & Klaus, R.A. (1982). *From three to twenty. The Early Training Project.* Baltimore, Ma: University Park Press.

Greist,D.L., Forehand, R., & Wells, K.C. (1981) Follow-up assessment of parental behavioral training: an analysis of who will participate, *Child Study Journal,* **11,** 221-229.

Hess, R.D., Kaswagi, K., Azuma, H., Price, D.G. & Dickson, W.P. (1980) Maternal expectations for mastery of developmental tasks in Japan and the United States. *International Journal of Psychology,* **15,** 259-271.

Hetzel, B.S. (1986) Mental defect due to iodine deficiency: a major international public health problem that can be eradicated. In Berg, J.M. (Ed.) *Science and Service in Mental retardation.* London: Methuen.

Holland, F.L.U. & Noaks, J.C. (1982). Portage in mid- Glamorgan. *Journal of the Association of Educational Psychologists,* **5,** 32-37.

Jesian, G., Aliaga, J. & Llanos, M. (1979) *Validation of the Portage model in Peru.* Paper presented at the International Congress of Psychology, Lima, Peru.

Jewell, T. & Brookes, M. (1984). *Leeds Portage Project : 1983/1984. Final evaluation report. Unpublished typescript.*

Kasiwagi, K., Azuma, H. & Miyake, K. (1982) Early maternal influence upon later cognitive development among Japanese children: a follow-up study. *Japanese Psychology Review,* **24,** 94-100

Keller, H., Miranda, D. & Guada, G. (1984) The naive theory of the infant and some maternal attitudes: a two country study. *Journal of Cross-Cultural Psychology,* **15,** 165-179.

Kholi, T. (1986) *Portage: progress, problems and possibilities in India.* Paper presented to the National Portage Conference, Winchester, England.

Kholi, T. & Datta, R. (1984) Portage Service: an intervention programme for preschool mentally retarded children with mental handicaps. *Punjab University Research Bulletin (Arts),* 15, 71-89.

Land, A. (1983) Portage - parents' news. *Educational Psychology in Practice,* **1,** 120-123.

Landau, R. (1982) Infant crying and fussing: findings from a cross-cultural study. *Journal of Cross-Cultural Psychology,* **13,** 427-444.

Lazar, I. & Darlington, R.B. (1982) Lasting effects of early education: a report from the Consortium of Longitudinal Studies. *Monographs of the Society of Research in Child Development,* **47,** (2-3). Social Number 195.

Ludlow, J.R. & Allen, L.M. (1979) The effects of early intervention and preschool stimulus on the development of the Down's Syndrome child. *Journal of Mental Deficiency Research,* **23,** 29-44.

Macmillan, D.L. & Turnbull, A.P. (1983) Parent involvement with special education: respecting individual preferences. *Education and Training of the Mentally Retarded,* **18,** 4-9.

Myatt, R. (1983) *Report of the independent evaluation of the South Lakeland Pre-school Advisory Service for the Westmoreland Society for the mentally handicapped.* Exeter University : Unpublished report.

Otaki, M., Durrett, M.E., Richards, P., Nyquist, L. & Pennybaker, J.W. (1986) National and infant behaviour in Japan and America: a partial replication. *Journal of Cross-Cultural Psychology,* **17,** 251-268.

Painter, L. (1986) *Portage-based services for Aukland, New Zealand.* Paper presesnted at the National Portage Conference, Winchester, England.

Penniston, E. (1972) *An evaluation of the Portage Project 1971-1972. Unpublished typescript.*

Quirk, M., Ciottone, R., Minami, H., Wapner,S., Tanomoto, T., Ishii, S., Lucca-Irizarry, N. & Pacheco, A. (1986) Values mothers hold for handicapped and non-handicapped preschool children in Japan, Puerto Rico and the United States mainland. *International Journal of Psychology,* **21,** 463-485.

Ramey, C.T. & Suarez, T.N. (1985) Early intervention and the early experience paradigm: toward a better framework for social policy. *Journal of Children in Contemporary Society,* **17,** 3-13.

Richardson, S.A. (1984) The consequences of malnutrition for intellectual development. In Dobbing, J., Clarke, A.D.B., Corbett, J.A., Hogg, J. and Robinson, R.O. (Eds.). *Scientificstudiesinmentalretardation.* London: RoyalSocietyofMedicine and MacMillan.

Sandow, S. & Clarke, A.D.B. (1978) Home intervention of parents of severely subnormal, pre-school children: an interim report. *Child: Care, Health and Development,* **4,** 29-39.

Sandow, S., Clarke, A.D.B., Cox, M.W. & Stewart, F.L. (1981) Home intervention with parents of severely subnormal pre-school children: a final report. *Child: Care, Health and Development,* **7,** 135- 144.

Shand, N. & Kosawa, Y. (1985) Japanese and American behaviour types at three months: infant and infant-mother dyads. *Infant Behavior and Development,* **8,** 225-240.

Shearer, D. & Ghazaleh, H.A. (1986) *The mother's home care early intervention outreach program in Ghaza.* Paper presesnted to the National Portage Conference, Winchester.

Shearer, D.E. & Loftin, C.R. (1984) The Portage project: teaching parents to teach their preschool children in the home. In Dangel, R.F. and Polster, R.A. (Eds.) *Parent training: foundations of research and practice.* London: Wilford.

Shearer, M.S. & Shearer, D.E. (1972) The Portage Project: a model for early childhood education. *Exceptional Children,* **36,** 210-217.

Sinha, S.R. (1985) Maternal strategies for regulating children's behaviour. *Journal of Cross-Cultural Psychology,* **16,** 27-40.

Smith, J., Kushlick, A. & Glossop, C. (1977) *The Wessex Portage Project: a home teaching service for families with a pre-school mentally handicapped child. Volume 1: Report. Volume II: Appendices.* University of Southampton: Health Care Evaluation Research Team.

Spitz, H.H. (1986a) *The raising of intelligence : a selected history of attempts to raise retarded intelligence.* Hillside, New Jersey: Lawrence Erbalum.

Spitz, H.H. (1986b) Preventing and curing mental retardation by behavioural intervention: an evaluation of some claims. *Intelligence,* **10,** 197-207.

Sturmey, P. & Crisp, A.G. (1986) Portage Guide to Early Education: a review of research. *Educational Psychology,* **6,** 139-157.

Syed, R. (1986) *A Question of cultural differences · Portage and Asian families.* Unpublished paper presented in the 10th National Portage Conference. Winchester, England. September 1986.

Turnbull, A.P. & Turnbull, H.R. (1982) Parent involvement in the education of handicapped children: a critique. *Mental Retardation,* **20,** 115-122.

White, K., & Casto, G. (1985) An integration review of early intervention efficacy studies with at risk children : implications for the handicapped. *Analysis and Intervention in Developmental Disabilities,* **5,** 7-32.

Winston, P. & Turnbull, P. (1981) Parent involvement as viewed by parents of pre-school handicapped children. *Topics in Early Childhood Special Education,* **1,** 11-19.

Wishart, M., Bidder, R. & Gray, O. (1980) Parental responses to their delayed children and the South Glamorgan home advisory service. *Child: Care, Health and Development,* **6,** 361-371.

Woods, P.A., Corney, M.J. & Pryce, G.J. (1984) Developmental progress of preschool Down's Syndrome children receiveing a home-advice service: interim report. *Child: Care, Health and Development,* **10,** 287-299.

Wolfendale, S. (1985) A review of parental involvement and the place of Portage. In Daly, B., Addington, J., Kerfoot, S. and Sigston, A. (Eds) *Portage: the importance of parents.* Windsor, Berkshire: NFER-Nelson.

Yamaguchi, K. (1986) *The Japanese adaptation of the Portage early intervention model and some results.* Unpublished paper presented at the 10th National Portage Confer-

CHAPTER 12

Unifying Services for Children With Mental Handicaps*

Euan Ross

Consultant Paediatrician, Riverside Health Authority, London, UK

INTRODUCTION

The need to make special provisions for the handicapped is self-evident and their quality is a good measure of a nation's civilisation. Such provision does not wholly depend on the gross national product but includes the quality of public attitudes towards the handicapped; these have to be voiced loudly before politicians will unlock public money. This requires a freely accessible media and a democratic regime. The people must also be willing to give of their time and to encourage their young to train for the caring professions at public expense. These concepts have to be taught and are not automatically found either in newly rich countries where the unproductive have traditionally been cast out, nor are they well developed under communist regimes. The present increasing British shortage of such personnel reflects a composite of relatively poor pay, lack of affordable accommodation in Southern cities and a changing perception towards rewards for vocational work.

One significant development of recent decades has been the near exponential increase in influence of voluntary societies for the handicapped. Although they arise in an unregulated manner and overlap each other, their record of achievement in developing public awareness, forcing political action and raising hard cash both for amelioration of hardship and support of research has been the single greatest advance. There is now a society with specific interests

*The author is grateful to his many colleagues who are currently, or have been in the past, associated with the National Child Development Study both at the National Children's Bureau and at the Institute of Child Health, London. He is also grateful to clinical colleagues especially Dr S. Jazeel, Principal Physician in Child Health, Riverside Health District, London, for inspiring advice over school health issues.

in most of the major identifiable handicaps of childhood as well as the large societies for handicap as a whole. Perhaps the most important aspect has been the development of a voice for parents together with the concept that parents are the conductors of their child's life and that their needs may be quite different from those perceived by their professional advisers.

RESEARCH RELEVANT TO SERVICE DEVELOPMENTS

There has been plenty of advice concerning the improvement of services for the handicapped from official government sponsored enquiries in recent years; well known sources include the Court report (1976) and its sequel ten years later (1987), the Warnock Report (1978), The Fish report (1985) into the future of special education in Inner London. To these are added numerous reports from voluntary and collaborative bodies such as the National Children's Bureau. A great deal of factual information about the state of child health education and social conditions has been gained both from intensive local studies starting with the post-war Newcastle 1000 family survey, by Miller et al. (1974), the Isle of Wight study of all school children on that island by Rutter, Graham and Yule (1972) and the specific study of epilepsy in children attending normal schools in Bedfordshire, by Holdsworth and Whitmore (1974).

The most complete British national overview of mental handicap in unselected school children comes from the National Child Development Study (N.C.D.S.) in which the ante- and perinatal histories of virtually all 17,733 children born in the week 3- 9 March 1958 in England, Scotland and Wales were documented. The survivors were traced to their schools at ages 7, 11 and 16 where they were medically examined, school performance assessed and parents visited by health visitors who recorded their socio-medical histories. The techniques used and a summary of the findings were published by Davie et al. (1972) and updated in edited form by Fogelman (1983). At 23 the cohort was again traced to their homes and socio-medical interviews undertaken.

Further British information about child development from unselected cohort samples comes from the two other national studies based on all children born in England, Scotland and Wales in single weeks in the spring of 1946, Douglas (1964, 1970); Butler and Golding (1986); much further data about the ability of school children with mental handicap are awaited from the latter study. Extrapolating from the findings of the studies based on the N.C.D.S.

1958 and 1970 births followed up in the Child Health and Development Study, it is clear that many school children with mental handicap in the United Kingdom have unfilled special needs. It is most unfortunate that the tradition of conducting them on a 12 yearly basis has now been broken, if another is not undertaken soon the hard won skills built up in this field will be lost. Such studies do not need to be all embracing, there is no necessity to study minutiae, the broad brush strokes are all that is required. So far there has been no alternative proposed that can replace this type of study, which brings medical, educational and sociological research together.

One of the steps urgently needed is to put the skills of market research and sampling that are so highly developed in commercial practice into ascertaining priority needs of the handicapped and the effectiveness of therapies. Those who take a special interest in mental handicap and its amelioration are hampered by a lack of accessible hard data against which to measure the results of differing forms of management. Not every claim for increased or special allocation of resources, however skillfully promoted, can or always should be afforded. Developments of new drugs, operations and management procedures all require testing. Controversial recent examples include late abortion and preventive treatments for fetal abnormality such as dietary supplementation, cosmetic surgery for Down's syndrome, keratoplasty for severe myopia, and marrow transplantation in the treatment of mucopolysaccharide disorder. Unless new procedures are tested before widescale introduction there are bound to be subsequent claims that in certain instances they can cause harm; ultrasound prenatal examination and immunisations are good examples.

Epidemiologically it is difficult to prove a negative and much better to undertake such investigations before a procedure is made freely available. Sometimes a particular form of therapy captures headlines, as in the case of conductive education. Although it has achieved the public relations dream of gaining vast media publicity at minimal cost it still waits assessment under British conditions, its methods first need to be divided into component parts and submitted to controlled studies.

The optimal care for children with mental handicap demands firstly that they receive the normal provision that all children require supplemented by support akin to bereavement counselling that families need when they learn that their infant is not the one they expected whether planned or not, laboured for and fantasised over. When the phase of high dependency is prolonged a range of extra needs becomes apparent. Those involved may cover the whole span of the child related professions and many others who would not conventionally be regarded as part of a child care team.

PERSONNEL

Medical and related personnel. A vast array of health service based personnel from many disciplines are involved in the care of mentally retarded children. Each group have their own training, professional loyalties and management structures, these include:

Nurses: on the hospital ward and outpatients, health visitors, school nurses, liaison nurses and specialists.

Therapists: e.g. music, occupational, play, physio, psycho, speech.

Dieticians, dental technicians and hygienists.

Clinical psychologists: e.g. diagnostic, programme planning and treatment of behaviour problems.

Administrators of a wide hierarchy of grades: secretaries and receptionists.

Appliance fitters. Opticians. Technicians.

Clinical investigators: Electroencephalography (E.E.G.), X- ray, clinical measurement, pathology, audiology, orthoptic.

Clinicians: audiologists, family doctors, ophthalmologists, orthopaedic and neurosurgeons, specialists in paediatrics who subdivide into school doctors, hospital and community based consultants, handicap specialists, neurologists, psychiatrists, dentists.

Social services both in the local authority special services, which acts as supportive agencies to statutory organisations and a host of voluntary bodies, many of which are at least in part supported by public funds. Such agencies rely greatly on a network of supportive staff who include home helps, child minders and foster parents.

Education. Although most handicapped children are educated in the maintained sector a sizeable added contribution comes from private schools which are mainly run through charitable bodies though some are commercial establishments. Their entire staff which include educational welfare and educational psychologists are part of a team which must closely overlap with social and medical services. The greatest problems of overlap and duplication arise where children are placed outwith their own local authority or in a privately run school which is not in receipt of local services.

PREMISES

In smaller towns the system is relatively straightforward and the best integration comes when professional staff have tenured posts and tend to stay long enough to get to know and trust the vast number of professional "opposite numbers" in their vicinity. Building up such a network takes at least two years and it is important that new staff particularly at a senior level have carefully worked out induction schemes. In the large towns there is endless opportunity for muddle between health districts and overlapping services. Family doctors have the right to refer patients to the most appropriate specialist or other hospital based service. In large cities there is often a wealth of poorly coordinated hospital based services and families may be able to indulge in the luxury of 'specialist hopping', something unknown to rural areas where it may be very difficult to get to any service at all. This practice is particularly common among better off parents who have immigrated from countries where it is conventional practice to seek multiple professional opinions before eventually settling temporarily with the most comfortable even if least appropriate one.

Increasingly the development of intensive regional units is posing the dilemma of maximal expertise at one point at the expense of increased travel for many. In many instances it is only possible to provide first rate treatment if services are concentrated into a few centres where enough experience and a large enough trained staff can be generated to build up real expertise and justify the equipment and support services needed.

CHILD DEVELOPMENT CENTRES

The creation of local truly interdisciplinary child development centres has been one of the most successful means of unifying services. By creating one, a health district brings together the wide range of therapists involved with child handicap work and the multiplicity of doctors. Ideally such a centre should make it possible for children to have their initial diagnostic assessment carried out under one roof in a short period. It is easy to bring staff together for conferences, a key worker can be selected and a unified and agreed pattern of continuing therapy can be drawn up. It is possible to write treatment plans, parents have the opportunity to get to know others in similar situations. In theory this sounds the answer to many needs but there are pitfalls. It is easier for staff to work in centres and the tendency for them not to visit schools, clinics and homes must be resisted.

The centre must not be seen as an ivory-towered institution, but a homely centre, and a balance has to be kept between heavy concentration of resources on a few families and spread of the budgetary cake among the larger number of children with lesser handicaps but great need for services who must be cared for in the community. It is also important that parents are not intimidated or 'deskilled' by the high level of expertise of the professional worker. Case conferences or discussions can be a major burden on parents who can feel threatened by large groups of professional workers.

Some questions must be answered - does every district need a centre, where should they be sited, how staffed ? Do district handicap teams as envisaged in the Court report really work - some districts never created one, some had them and disbanded them - are they a practical entity? My experience suggests that such teams if skillfully chaired and well backed up by good clerical support are a very effective way of ensuring that senior staff from the child-centred disciplines in an overlapping health and local government authority build up an effective means of working together. For these teams to be cost effective they must be kept small, have a clearly defined brief and evaluate their own effectiveness. They should not become 'mini case conferences', their main function is to ensure that medical, social and educational services know the local children with present or forthcoming special educational needs. They can ensure that 'statementing' is started in plenty of time and that the right disciplines are asked to contribute. I do not see how the 1981 Education Act can be effectively implemented without one. Their creation has given rise to two problems: first, these teams can absorb a great deal of time in discussion, it is important that the fact finding is done before hand; secondly, individual workers may resent the fact that 'their' children are being discussed without their presence. To bring them in, however, alters the whole tenor of the teams' working. These teams are not there to make clinical decisions about the child's care.

A great deal of local education is needed to ensure that the roles of the team are clearly understood. Establishing a computer based handicap register which records the fact that necessary work has been done on each appropriate child greatly strengthens the scope of the team. There is an enormous variation between the services provided by seemingly similar districts. This is revealed by the great variations in proportions of children 'statemented' between seemingly similar authorities.

UNIFYING SERVICES

Despite the prominence given to shortages in health, social and educational services it remains possible to overload a child and family with services and tasks to fulfill. All professional experts must repeatedly ask themselves - does this child really need my services. Through my action am I 'deskilling' the family. Could they learn the task and do it themselves? All too often children are discharged from a clinic with an invitation to come back if necessary, yet do not perceive the need for a return visit. Unfortunately many parents have diffculty in judging that moment. Further questions that must be asked include - Can my service or therapy be done at school? Can I teach the parents the skill? If the child comes from another authority's territory (teaching health districts please note) are there suitable services available in the child's own locality that are being overlooked. If I take on this distant child am I reducing the services available and funded for local children?

There is a clear need for a central organisation to promote and facilitate the coordination of services for the handicapped and encourage good practice. This is not something that government departments can do on their own. Concerted pressure from the professions is needed. One suggestion is to develop a national organisation that could promote standards along the lines of the British Association for Adoption and Fostering.

HOW EFFECTIVE IS STAFF TRAINING?

Interdisciplinary teaching remains a rarity. Although an attractive concept it requires great effort to get various groups of students from various disciplines into the same room at the same time. Syllabuses vary and educational levels and standards vary. There is however much waste in the National Health Service (NHS) where medical and nursing libraries, classrooms and audiovisual equipment are kept rigidly separate. Often the same classroom teaching would be relevant to a wide variety of students. One of the problems from the medical side is that all teaching is done by those who have other fully absorbing duties and very little time in which to plan curricula. The medical curriculum time has not been increased in the past 100 years whilst the amount of knowledge and practical skill required has vastly increased. Every subject jostles with others in a market place of clinical teaching time. Medical students are highly realistic in their assessment of the weight that a subject may carry in the examinations.

SOME DIFFICULT AND THREATENING SOLUTIONS

The current controversy about the role of conductive education for children with cerebral palsy has reopened the concept of the multifunction therapist who can function as speech, physio and occupational therapist in one highly trained being and among doctors the idea of a 'handicapologist' with a high degree of skill in a number of paediatric fields including audiology, ophthalmology, psychology, genetics and neurology. Is it worth pressing for this? Such doctors have started to emerge in the UK though the concept is better developed in Scandinavia where they are known as 'habilitationalists'. These are the key skills of a consultant community paediatrician, the creation of which was one of the recommendations of the Court report proposals that are being implemented - about one third of health authorities now have at least one in post but large districts, particularly those in inner cities need at least two so there is a large gap yet to fill. These paediatricians bring fuller experience in the diagnosis and treatment of handicap to the child health services than was available in the past. The expectation is that the medical supervision of handicapped children can be undertaken in a much more coordinated fashion than when specialist medical services were divided between hospital paediatric departments and community services. Hopefully the advent of university based MSc courses will help to ensure there are enough suitably trained candidates for these posts, though financial support ot trainees will have to be made available.

There are too few child neurologists in the UK to provide an ongoing service for children with mental handicap. Rightly their efforts have to be put into the diagnosis and treatment of the rarer neurological problems that are best managed in hospital. Child psychiatry is often practised in isolation from other branches of paediatrics resulting in needless separation of two closely related forms of paediatric practice which would give a more useful service if they were more closely integrated through common training, premises and resources.

CARE OF THE CARERS

Media led attacks on professional staff involved in child care and protection has had the unfortunate effect of damaging the status of these professions which already suffer the disadvantage of lower levels of pay and poorer working conditions than have come to be the norm for professional people. Working environmnents are the clearest demonstration of the regard in which employers hold their employees. Every service needs a pyramidal structure whereby the most gifted and energetic can rise to top positions whilst remaining active in the provision of services rather than as administrators. The dangers of this have been clearly evident in nursing where the only route to a high position has involved renouncing actual "hands on" nursing.

HANDING OVER

Although special education can be extended to age 19, leaving school often coincides with handover of specialist medical care from paediatricians to adult centred services and much family support is lost simultaneously. The whole burden of care for the young person with handicapping disorder may be thrown back on to now aging parents. For those who are even mildly handicapped job finding is difficult and only those who received a good enough education will be in a favourable position. For many with continuing mental handicap but who have not been taught marketable skills, employment prospects are bleak.

CONCLUSIONS

Optimal care is only possible when parents, teachers and older children have a clear understanding about the nature of the child's particular form of handicap, the rationale of treatment and prognosis. Whilst the diagnosis is a medical responsibility it is vital that other members of the team, particularly health visitors, clearly understand the condition and can accurately reinforce doctors' explanations to parents. Analysis of questions sent in by subscribers to a nursing journal demonstrates that many readers do not have access to understandable textbooks nor feel it easy to discuss conditions with medical specialists. In a growing child, problems, symptoms and social needs can readily change and periodic re-examination and reassessment are needed throughout childhood.

The best management occurs when there is close team-work between parents, doctors, schoolteachers, nurses and therapists from many disciplines. Although levels of provision for the handicapped child in many parts of the UK are not adequate, parents can be overwhelmed by too much therapeutic zeal. There remains much to be done before we can begin to talk about optimal management and true unification of services for handicapped children. Although rightly the major scientific thrusts in the immediate future will be on the prevention of handicap, even partial elimination remains a far distant prospect and conditions acquired by accident will be always with us. The techniques needed to deliver much improved services are largely available already, the requirement now is for their delivery to all those who need them.

REFERENCES

Butler, N.R. & Golding, J. (1986) *From Birth to Five.* Oxford: Pergamon Press.

Davie R., Butler N.R. & Goldstein, H. (1972) *From Birth to Seven.* London: Longman.

Douglas, J.W.B. (1964) *The Home and the School.* London: MacGibbon & Kee.

Education Act (1981) London: HMSO.

Fish, J. (1985) *Educational Opportunities for All.* ILEA: Inner London Education Authority.

Fit for the Future (1976) *The Report of the Committee on Child Health Services. (The Court report).* London: HMSO.

Holdsworth, L. & Whitmore, K. (1974) A study of children with epilepsy attending ordinary schools. 1: Their seizure patterns, progress and behaviour in school. *Developmental Medicine and Child Neurology,* **16,** 746 - 758.

Miller, F.J.W., Court, S.D.M., Knox, E.G. & Brandon, S. (1974) *The School Years in Newcastle upon Tyne.* Oxford: Oxford University Press.

Rutter, M., Graham, P. & Yule, W. (1972) *A Neuropsychiatric Study in Childhood.* London: Spastics International Medical Publications.

Warnock, M. (1978) *Special Educational Needs: report of Committee of Enquiry into the Education of Handicapped Children and Young People.* London: HMSO.

Investing in the Future. Child Health Ten Years after the Court Report. (1987) London: National Children's Bureau.

CHAPTER 13

Epilogue

Alan Clarke

Department of Psychology, University of Hull, UK

Peter Evans

Department of Child Development and Educational Psychology, University of London Institute of Education, London, UK

INTRODUCTION

Research in mental retardation is to be found in three very broad areas; to some extent these overlap and are interdependent. First, *precise description* of groups, sub- groups or individuals is required, whether at cytological, somatic, psychological or social levels. Second, *aetiological research* may lead to primary or secondary preventive measures. These embrace a wide range of possibilities, including immunization against childhood diseases which can have neurological *sequelae,* pre-natal diagnosis, ante-natal care and peri-natal monitoring, surgery for some forms of hydrocephalus and social intervention for the child at risk of mild retardation associated with disadvantage. Primary prevention, of course, seeks to avoid subsequent retardation; secondary prevention aims to overcome already existing, or developing, handicaps. As such it shades into, thirdly, *amelioration* of retardation by optimising or creating skills in the individual. This book has been concerned with all three approaches, and its contents have been reflected in the title.

All scientific disciplines bearing upon the human condition have contributed to the major advances in our understanding of the causes, prevention and treatment of mental retardation. In this connection, post-war developments, have been of special historical interest. The first edition of Penrose's *Biology of Mental Defect* (1949) was largely descriptive, and only one chapter out of twelve was explicitly concerned with treatment. Although prevention was implied in parts of the book, even genetic counselling is omitted from the index. Yet Penrose's influence was immense, and he laid the foundations for later advances. Similarly the first volume on mental retardation by a psychologist in the post-war years (Sarason, 1949) was again mainly descriptive, devoting only one chapter out of ten to treatment or amelioration.

During the 1950s, the situation began to change radically as more and more scientific information became available. During that decade questions of prevention and amelioration became prominent (Penrose, 1954; Hilliard and Kirman, 1957; Clarke and Clarke, 1958). In the last book, for example, seven chapters out of eighteen were directly concerned with amelioration.

In brief the foundations for nearly all of the more recent advances were laid in the 1950s and 1960s. At the same time, strong pressures from parents' groups combined with this new knowledge, forced radical changes in official attitudes, services and expectancies of what could be done for the retarded. Many of these were reflected in the Mental Health Act of 1959 which replaced the repressive practices of the 1913 Mental Deficiency Act.

During this whole period the recognition that mental retardation posed multi-disciplinary problems began to take hold. Thus in 1960 the first international multi-disciplinary congress on the "scientific study of mental retardation" was held in London, to be followed four years later in Copenhagen by the foundation of an International Association of that name. It became clear that no single profession holds the key to this subject and thus multi-disciplinary collaboration is increasingly necessary.

OVERVIEW

A brief synopsis of the major arguments advanced in this book will now be offered. Following an introduction to the general issues, chapters two and three have addressed epidemiological problems that spring from issues concerned with the definition and identification of mentally retarded children and adults as well as from methodological sources. It is not perhaps surprising that the epidemiological picture that emerges is immensely complex. This stems in part from the over-simple views about definition, measurement and the assumed solely biological nature of the problem that has been taken in the past. Nowadays, of course, we recognise the importance, albeit inexactly, of social factors in the aetiology of some forms of mental retardation and difficulties in social adaptation are now included in the definition. However, for those conditions where social influences may account for a greater proportion of the variance, and which include many cases of mild mental retardation (MMH), Richardson has wondered whether the concept of MMH "has outlived its usefulness". This view is also shared by Fryers who is equally concerned that it is now not justifiable to treat mental retardation as an "epidemiological unity". For both authors the future holds interest in more detailed individual studies or group studies where biological (e.g. genetic) causes are known definitely to exist.

The next two chapters, by Alberman and by Baumeister, take up issues relating to primary and secondary prevention. Alberman sticks closely to a medical orientation, indicating what can be achieved in primary prevention, strictly defined, through improved nutrition, genetic counselling and the prevention of potential damage. She also discusses prevention (not strictly primary) that comes about through identification of anomalies that will often lead to termination and finally some aspects of secondary prevention (e.g. treatment, after birth, of PKU).

Many of the issues are taken up in some length by Baumeister who argues that mental retardation is but one symptom of the "new morbidity". This is a general set of conditions stemming from a complex interaction between biological, behavioural and cultural variables. He claims that we are witnessing a dramatic increase in such problems as learning disability and behaviour difficulties as well as childhood mental disorder, murder and suicide. Baumeister and his colleagues have developed a complex model to help to conceptualise the issues. In this model, limited personal and social resources, poverty and demographic factors, behavioural and genetic/biological aspects come together to increase the likelihood of the "new morbidity". Overcoming such problems would in principle help to serve both primary and secondary preventive functions.

The importance of social and environmental factors in both understanding children described as being mentally retarded and ameliorating their problems has been pointed out in the first chapter of this book. The significance of these influences has, of course, always been of importance to educationalists and the issues have been taken up in the next five chapters. Gulliford traces the history of education for pupils with moderate learning difficulties (MLD) and argues that the changes in terminology that have occurred, by replacing the category of educationally subnormal with the descriptive label of MLD is more than just a change in label but reflects a shift in the conceptualisation of the problem. It carries with it a recognition of a number of practical implications such as integration and classroom support in contrast to segregation and withdrawal. However, Cline's analysis of the content of "Statements" made on pupils in fulfillment of the 1981 Education Act reveals that it is not easy to abandon ideas of the fixed IQ in our understanding of the functioning of these children and that the place and purpose of the LEA's special school for MLD pupils is virtually unchanged.

Much discussion of schooling tends to assume that all schools are the same. The chapter by Evans, Redmond and Ireson describes qualitative methods used to compare ten MLD schools. Their analysis shows striking differences in the way these schools operate and they argue that some forms of organisation are better able to provide effective amelioration and secondary prevention than others. The functioning of one such school, based on a skills analysis model, is described in some detail by Robertshaw. The account reveals how a school can modify its curriculum to meet the needs of pupils as they arise, as well as providing appropriate subject based education.

The themes of all these chapters are echoed in chapter 10 by Richardson, Koller and Katz. In this the difficulties of understanding the term MLD are highlighted in the context of their longitudinal study in Aberdeen which has followed through MLD pupils who have left school, some of whom are now at work. A number of important and complex issues are raised by this chapter. These focus the attention on questions that relate to definition and classification and point to the heterogeneity of the membership of the MLD grouping which has inappropriately, in the past, effectively been treated as an aetiological entity. This chapter highlights the "six-hour retardate syndrome" (e.g. see Garber, 1988) and begins to develop the school-based themes, referred to earlier, into the work setting; namely the necessity to change the working conditions to meet the needs of children described as MLD as a form of amelioration.

The penultimate two chapters in this book by Sturmey and by Ross consider the effectiveness of services. Sturmey discusses Portage, a pre-school programme to help parents to develop skills in their mentally retarded children. He points out that there is still much to be done in evaluating its effects. However, cross-cultural experience suggests that to understand the factors associated with effective intervention it is necessary to consider the more complex patterns of relationship that exist within families. Two issues are of especial significance. These are the family's expectations about children's development and their place in the particular culture concerned.

In an expansion of this ecological thinking Ross considers the need to unify services in order to achieve the most effective provision for mentally retarded people. We have already seen the multitude of services that a child may receive (Robertshaw, Chapter 9, Table 6) and there is obviously a need to integrate their activities if total intervention is to be achieved.

In overviewing the various contributions to this volume it is clear that almost all of the chapters point to the need to appreciate more fully the complex array of variables which, when identified, might ultimately allow us to understand better the causes of mental retardation. It is clear that traditional approaches, while of great value, need to be extended within a systems/ecological framework. This requires multi-disciplinary collaboration of an organised sort. The need for the existence of such locally organised systems has been heralded over the past 10 to 15 years; perhaps the next ten will see their realisation. It is clear that significant further progress in our understanding of handicapping conditions and of the new morbidities together with their prevention and amelioration will be considerably hampered without such exciting developments.

THE FUTURE

Prediction of future research trends is hazardous; some initial discoveries may be serendipitous yet lead to major revolutions in knowledge. Yet others exploit existing findings and advance logically step-by-step; in these cases future trends are more easily anticipated. In this section some obvious fields for further investigation are outlined.

In the biomedical area, further and rapid advances in understanding the genetics of some forms of mental retardation are to be expected. For example, very recent evidence has pin-pointed the location of the gene for tuberous sclerosis on the distal long arm of chromosome 9, and further work on gene mapping will show high promise (Fryer et al., 1987). Premature aging in Down's syndrome has been shown to be related to Alzheimer's Disease, involving chromosome 21 (St Clair, 1987). genetic engineering recombination techniques are likely to be important for prevention (Dudgeon, 1984), and it is also probable that further aetiological discoveries will make inroads on what has been regarded as the large group of "undifferentiated" severe and in some cases mild retardation. For example, the discovery of the fragile X chromosome (Lubs, 1969) has revealed the second largest aetiological group after Down's syndrome.

There is likely to be more widespread usage of the various non-invasive brain imaging techniques (CAT - Computerized Axial Tomography, PET - Positron Emission Tomography, NMR - Nuclear Magnetic Resonance) which will shed light not only on the nature and extent of brain lesions and malformations, together with their behavioural correlates, but also provide images of *in vivo* brain functioning (Rutter, 1986)

For the severely retarded, we already know that most behavioural processes are modifiable, sometimes only minimally, sometimes quite dramatically. Both laboratory and "real life" experiments have demonstrated this for particular skills. but all these represent far less than total intervention. This latter word has become omnibus in character, describing, on the one hand, brief periods over a few weeks and on the other, early or late adoption. A careful prospective, wide-ranging and very lengthy developmental study is needed to gain some idea of the range of individual limits to improvement. Until these are known, the accepted possibilities for helping the severely retarded are likely to be too modest. Cunningham's (1987) prospective two year intervention from birth with a large group of Down's children and their parents have no measurable long-term effects, although it gave parents considerable satisfaction. Cunningham himself wonders whether changes in child rearing may have made his type of intervention redundant. There may well be a secular trend in early childhood for better development. There are, however, a few straws in the wind for more total intervention. A number of clinicians have noticed that a very unusual Down's child invariably comes from a home where the mother is a teacher, nurse or suchlike (e.g. Gath, 1987).

The present period witnesses some radical changes in service provision in the light of policies for de-institutionalization, integration in schools and, in general, normalization in the lives of the mentally retarded. Differing approaches and differing facilities occur naturally, and provide the possibility for *independent* evaluation, for cost benefit and other comparative studies. In this way, models of good practice may be built up. More knowledge is badly needed on exactly what can be done, for what sort of person, from what type of home context and by what sort of methods.

The forms of intervention commonly used for the severely or mildly retarded produce, at the best, immediate and significant results, but much less impressive long-term outcomes unless reinforcing situations powerfully operate, e.g. as in some schools, from the end of intervention and onwards. For milder cases, there is considerable doubt whether radical improvements can be induced when the person remains in the social conditions associated in the first place with the problem. A few studies indicate that ecological change can have marked effects. Most investigations of brief preschool interventions (e.g. Head Start) have been concerned with disadvantaged children, and hence, with the mentally retarded in a minority. For the latter one would expect poorer learning and poorer retention of that learning from enriched experiences. Once again, more lengthy and wide-ranging interventions need to be prospectively planned, including especially those where total ecological change has occurred. Where the latter does not take place, there needs to be an evaluation of whether family constellations are, as one suspects, more resistant to change than the mildly handicapped young member. Probably those parents with "severely deprived" children are overwhelmed by personal and material disadvantages and are thus unable to respond to help (Bronfenbrenner, 1974).

The general message to which future intervention research must address itself is whether only powerful and prolonged ecological change is likely to have potent long-term effects on the child who is potentially or actually retarded. In addition, which indicators of change at both individual and systems levels should we be looking for? There are a number of reports on the histories of adopted individuals, but group studies are rare. A recent French investigation is relevant. Children selected for low IQ (mean = 77) were adopted between ages four and six. On follow-up between 11 and 16, more than a quarter had IQ's above 100, a quarter remained retarded and the remaining half lay in between. The mean of the whole group was now 91, and scholastic achievements paralleled these findings (Duyme and Dumaret, 1986 and personal communication).

Further development of epidemiological studies may also be anticipated. There is probably now occurring a reduction in the incidence of some forms of severe retardation (eg by the immunization of adolescent girls against the rubella virus), counter-balanced by increasing longevity, so that overall prevalence rates remain roughly in balance. The impact of preventive measures and secular trends will need to be monitored. For the mildly retarded epidemiological findings have been bedevilled by the use of different criteria at different times and in different places. The Aberdeen study is a model for the future in that both psychometric and administrative measures were addressed separately and in combination. However, a greater hazard now faces epidemiologists, for some of the milder cases of school age will be located within the wider category of children with special educational needs. Where they can be identified, their progress under this new label and (possibly?) better services needs to be tracked.

Most psychiatrists and clinical psychologists have, naturally enough, been majorly concerned with the aetiology of breakdown, whether into mental illness or evolution into delinquency or mild retardation. They should be equally concerned with the process whereby some children appear to be invulnerable, resilient or stress resistant. From time to time authors have drawn attention to this important problem (e.g. Clarke and Clarke, 1960) but more recently empirical work has begun to shed light on these processes. Thus the inter- relationship between socio-economic status, maternal education and outcome are already the subject of investigation (Werner and Smith, 1981; Garmezy and Rutter, 1983). Moreover, the findings of Rutter et al., 1975, who studied the incidence of psychiatric disorder in children, is likely to generalise to many cases of mild retardation. Identifying some six risk factors, these authors showed that the presence of one yielded no greater incidence of disorder than occurred in risk-free controls. Two such factors had a multiplicative effect, resulting in a four-fold increase in risk, while four factors produced a ten-fold increase.

These, then, are just a few of the broad areas in description, prevention and amelioration to which future research is likely to address itself. Two major factors, however, now threaten the continuation of the major advances which have taken place during the last three or four decades. First, current social disruption and the diminution of unskilled employment opportunities are likely to increase the numbers of mildly retarded who will be identified administratively as exhibiting problems of social adaptation. They will be the least promising members of a new social underclass. Hence, the optimism generated by past prevalence studies, follow-up investigations and research upon delayed maturation, may no longer be justified. The second major casualty are the current restrictions on funding scientific research; this is regrettable on both humane and economic grounds. While applied research with short-term goals may be less damaged than "pure" research, ultimately it will be emasculated without progress in work upon fundamental or "basic" issues.

To summarise, this book has provided evidence upon the major issues of precise description of the retarded, and upon the aetiology of various forms of retardation, with consequent prospects of prevention, especially of the more severe conditions. It has also outlined various approaches to amelioration, in the context, in all these areas, of a growing interest in multi-disciplinary research. Advances in the last thirty years of study have vastly outweighed those from the whole history of previous knowledge in this field.

REFERENCES

Bronfenbrenner, U. (1974) *A Report on Longitudinal Evaluation of Preschool Programs*, Vol. 2, *Is Early Intervention Effective?* Washington, D.C.: DHEW Publication No. (OHD) 74-25.

Clarke, A. D. B. & Clarke, A. M. (1960) Some recent advances in the study of early deprivation. *Journal of Child Psychology and Psychiatry*, **1**, 26-36.

Clarke, A. M. & Clarke, A. D. B. (Eds.) (1958) *Mental Deficiency: the Changing Outlook*. London: Methuen.

Cunningham, C. (1987) Early intervention in Down's syndrome. In G. Hosking and G. Murphy (Eds.) *Prevention of Mental Handicap: A World View*. London: Royal Society of Medicine Services.

Dudgeon, J. A. (1984) Commentary. In J. Dobbing, A. D. B. Clarke, J. Corbett, J. Hogg and R. O. Robinson (Eds.) *Scientific Studies in Mental Retardation*. London: The Royal Society of Medicine and Macmillan.

Duyme, M. & Dumaret, A. (1986) La reversibilité de la débilité légère: une thérapeutique sans thérapeute. *CNAMS- INSERM*, **144,** 553-562.

Fryer, A. E., Chalmers, A., Connor, J. M., Fraser, I., Povey, S., Yates, A.D. & Osborne, J. P. (1987). Evidence that the gene for tuberous sclerosis is on chromosome 9. *Lancet*, **i,** 659-661.

Garber, H.L. (1988) *The Milwaukee Project*. Washington, DC: American Association on Mental Retardation

Garmezy, N. & Rutter M. (Eds.) (1983) *Stress, Coping and Development in Children*. New York: McGraw Hill.

Gath, A. (1987) Discussion. (p 169) In G. Hosking and G. Murphy (Eds.) *Prevention of Mental Handicap: A World View*. London: Royal Society of Medicine Services.

Hilliard, L. T. & Kirman, B. H. (1957) *Mental Deficiency*. London: J. and A. Churchill.

Lubs, H. A. (1969) A marker-X chromosome. *American Journal of Human Genetics*, **21,** 231-244.

Penrose, L. S. (1949, 1954) *The Biology of Mental Defect*. London: Sidgwick and Jackson.

Rutter, M. (1986) Child psychiatry: looking 30 years ahead. *Journal of Child Psychology and Psychiatry*, **27,** 803-840.

Rutter, M. Yule, B. Quinton, D., Rowlands, O., Yule, W. & Berger, M. (1975) Attainment and adjustment in two geographical areas: III. Some factors accounting for area differences. *British Journal of Psychiatry*, **126,** 520-533.

Sarason, S. B. (1949) *Psychological Problems in Mental Deficiency*. New York: Harper & Row.

St Clair, D. (1987) Chromosome 21, Down's syndrome and Alzheimer's Disease. *Journal of Mental Deficiency Research*, **31,** 213-214.

Werner, E. E. & Smith, R. S. (1981) *Vulnerable but Invincible: a Longitudinal Study of Resilient Children and Youth*. New York: McGraw Hill.

Subject Index

Author Index